LONG ODDS

by

DENIS G. LONG

CARTOONS by

'ROY' CALDERON

SKETCHES by

MARK C. M. LONG

LONG ODDS LTD., P.O.Box 2132, Hove, East Sussex, UK, BN3 8AQ.
© Denis G. Long 1996. The right of Denis G. Long to be identified as author of this work has been
asserted by him in accordance with the Copyright & Patents Act 1989.
First Published 1996. This book is set in Cheltenham.
Printed & bound by *TECHNIQUE* Colchester, Essex, England CO1 1HP

INTRODUCTION

This is a delightful insight, flavoured by a number of topical jokes and cartoons into the problems handled daily by your 'dedicated servants, 'the front line airline staff'. Mainly humerous anecdotes, some are rather sad.

Denis Long, whom I have known for many years, has spent two-thirds of his long career in overseas service and we are fortunate that his memory is so rich. What virtually inexhaustible fun we could have had, had he kept a diary.

Fortunately, he has sufficient material for two possibly three sequels, if you enjoy LONG ODDS and help make a success of it.

David A. Coltman.
Senior Vice President Marketing
 UNITED AIRLINES

FOREWORD

For over forty five years, I have enjoyed a fabulously interesting career, in Commercial Aviation. Never, did I know *That Monday Morning Feeling.*

Throughout, I have talked about comic and interesting incidents with colleagues and friends. Many urged me to write my autobiography and on the strength of their encouragement I began. I researched technique and learned, that unless one is famous or one invents something unique, don't bother. 'You will not even get inside a Publisher's Office'. Having recalled a couple of hundred anecdotes for the autobiography and having been recommended to read a recent best seller on Commercial Aviation anecdotes, I decided to scrap the autobiography and go for what follows. Most of what I have written is original, either experienced first hand by a colleague or myself. Some are 'industry stories' which because of re-telling change – remember the World War 1 'Send reinforcements, we are going to advance'. After many relays it reached H.Q as 'Send three and four pence we are going to a dance'. They are, nevertheless, retained for my non aviation readers.

My regret, is that I never kept a diary, I found the *business* version a drag. Thank God I have a reliable memory. Had I kept a diary, boy could I then have written some books!

While this is **not, nor was it intended to be,** a *Work of Literary Art,* telling an anecdote or joke is vastly different to writing it. Further, written grammatically correct takes much of the content away. Writing this has given me considerable pleasure, if it gives you half as much pleasure, I know that you will consider its purchase excellent value.

Friends have encouraged me to continue writing (I have over 500 more anecdotes on disc), if you have an anecdote of a Commercial Aviation flavour, I would appreciate hearing from you. If, after evaluation, it is included in a sequel, *full credit will be given to the contributor.*

Those interested, please write direct to **LONG ODDS,**
P.O.Box 2132, Hove, East Sussex , UK, BN3 8AQ.

My thanks go to all former colleagues, far too many to mention, who, throughout those 45 odd years, have been such an essential ingredient in the recipe of a tremendously satisfying career.

ACKNOWLEDGEMENTS

My 650 plus anecdotes have been collated over 45 years in Commercial Aviation. **LONG ODDS** contains approximately **217** anecdotes, jokes plus cartoons, photographs & sketches/maps. If you make its' publication a success, it will be followed by three more, titled **'LONGER ODDS', 'EVEN LONGER ODDS' & 'LONGEST ODDS'.**

My thanks go to all who have contributed, 'proof read' and evaluated, as well as those who have encouraged me. Amongst these are my wife Anne, my son Mark, Jerry Rycroft, Jim Churchman Bill Rothera, & David Taylor whose technical skills on the P.C-Word Processor made my writing so much easier.

My sincere thanks go to David A. Coltman of *UNITED AIRLINES* for his introduction, 'ROY' Calderon for his Cartoons, Mark Long *for his Sketches including the 'aircraft' towing titles along, UNITED AIRLINES, AIRBUS INDUSTRIES, SOUTHWEST AIRLINES, DENNIS FIRE ENGINES, ASIA AEROSPACE MAGAZINE, SOUTH AFRICAN AIRWAYS, and Brian Bradbury Photography I.o.W* for the use of their materials, which are in this or will be in the sequels.

CONTENTS

Anecdotes	Page

Anecdotes	**Page**

Anecdotes	Page

'ROY'

1921-1996

LONG ODDS is dedicated to 'ROY' Calderon who died while we were going to print.

Roy will be fondly remembered by me, my family and by all in Commercial Aviation who over many years, enjoyed his work. So much of which featured the now famous 'CALDERON *GIRLS*'.

Denis G. Long, Author.

A CALDERON *GIRL.*

UNACCOMPANIED MINO/ERS

They were already very uptight at Gatwick, their flight from Los Angeles had arrived late causing them to miss their connection to Lagos.

Offered an alternative routing via Paris or Rome, they preferred to night-stop at British Caledonian's expense, however the Agent looking after them would not agree.

They *demanded* to see the Duty Officer.

When told that they could not immediately see him, because he was sorting out a problem concerning a three unaccompanied **minors,** the businessmen nearly flipped.

One passenger, thinking that they were **miners,** sarcastically asked,

"What happened then, did the cage from the 9,000' level arrive late at the surface?" —————**MINORS?!!!**

"WE NEED YOUR TRAVELLERS' CHEQUES"

A Caledonian Airways (who joined B.U.A to form B.C.A.L.) B707 was en route from Oakland, California to Gatwick. Unusually strong headwinds were encountered and the commander decided that it would be prudent to make a fuelling call to 'top up' his tanks before the long over water flight.

He landed at Edmonton, Alberta Canada. After taking on every gallon his tanks would accept, the Captain presented his 'Carnet', to the Fuelling Officer. He took it to his office for processing. His Superintendent refused to accept it, 'Caledonian are on a cash basis' he said .

The Captain walked into the office, just in time to hear the bad news. "What on earth are you talking about, my company is financially sound" he insisted.

"Not any more, we received a telex only yesterday, clearly instructing us *CASH ONLY* from Caledonian. Can't locate it just now, but I clearly remember it" he was told. All arguments and protestations were to no avail. The superintendent went as far as instructing the airport police to ensure that the 707 was not allowed to depart, until the bill was paid.

The commander returned to his aircraft, where all 189 passengers had been re boarded. He explained their plight adding that the combined value of all crew members' Credit Cards, was insufficient to cover the cost of the fuel. If they would 'loan' the company their travellers' cheques, he guaranteed that they would be provided with replacements on landing at Gatwick. A number of passengers were unhappy but one wise gentleman pointed out,

a) They were at the start of their vacation.

b) He had no desire to spend his hard earned vacation at Edmonton, as much as he liked Canadians.

c) Since their aircraft, was 'on its way home', the company would be in the best position to reimburse them.

All on board offered their money. The crew very carefully noted passengers' name, Travellers Cheque numbers and the value of each 'contribution'. As soon as the captain could speak directly to Gatwick, he passed all details of his passengers' help.

As the passengers exited Customs, they were shepherded to an office, where each received a replacement set of travellers' cheques and a small gift of appreciation. They were shown a copy of the offending telex message warning the fuel company staff at every airport Caledonian Airways used. It read. 'A NEW CALEDONIA AIRLINE' (not Caledonian Airways), had financial difficulties.

 # THE EXECUTIVE JET

A Mid-East millionaire, who had a very elaborately furnished personal BAC 1-11 jet, approached B.C.A.L to contract his maintenance,

B.C.A.L was not keen to take on more outside engineering at present. They were not happy with the reputation of this particular individual on his debt payments.

Rather than offend and create 'political' difficulties, they out priced themselves by 300%.

Somewhat shocked, the owner asked who else could carry out such work. "Why, British Aircraft Corporation Weybridge, the manufacturers. No distance at all by air". The millionaire took off.

Next day he was back accepting B.C.A.L's offer. Puzzled, B.C.A.L Engineering unofficially talked to the British Aircraft Corporation. Having similar fears, they had quoted 500% above normal!

WHAT CARRIERS ARE REALLY CALLED

A number of airline names and/or initials have been 'modified' within and without the industry. Before getting to specifics, passengers with a grudge have been known to call any carrier XYZ SCAREWAYS. Royal Air Force Transport Command used to be ribbed "If you've time to spare, travel by air".

Alternative 'names' used world-wide are:

AERONAVES de MEXICO (as was)	AERO NERVOUS.
AIR FRANCE	AIR CHANCE.
AIR LANKA **(SRI LANKA)**	Always Intend Return *to* Land And Not Kill Anyone.
AIR NEW ZEALAND	AFTER NOVEMBER ZILCH.
AEROFLOT **(RUSSIA)**	AEROFLOP.
AER LINGUS	AIR FUNGUS.
ALITALIA	ALWAYS LATE IN TAKE OFF, ALWAYS LATE IN ARRIVAL.
AIR AFRIQUE	AIR TRAGIC.
ALL NIPON AIRWAYS	ALL NEW AVIATORS. ALL NIP-ON & ALL NIP-OFF.
AEROLINEAS ARGENTINAS **& AMERICAN AIRLINES**	ALCOHOLICS ANONYMOUS.
AIR 2,000	Is affectionately known as AIR two bob. AIR Dos Mille.
AIR U.K	AIR YUCH!
B.A.A **BRITISH AIRPORTS AUTHORITY**	BRITS AGAINST AVIATION.

B.C.A.L
(as was)

BETTER CRAWL ACROSS LOVER.

BRITISH EUROPEAN AIRWAYS
(as was)

BRITAIN'S EXCUSE for an AIRLINE.
BRITISH EXTRAORDINARY AIRWAYS.
BLOODY EXPENSIVE AIRLINE.

BRITISH ISLAND AIRWAYS
(as was)

BEWILDERING IN ACTION.

B.O.A.C
(as was)

BROTHERLY ORDER of
ANGLICAN CHURCHMEN.
BEND OVER AGAIN CHRISTINE.
BETTER ON A CAMEL.
BOOK ON ANOTHER CARRIER.
'B.O' AIRWAYS CORPORATION.
BE 'OME AFTER CHRISTMAS.

& B.C.A.L's favourite

BETTER OFF AT CALEDONIAN.

B.W.I.A
BRITISH WEST INDIES AIRWAYS
(TRINIDAD & TOBAGO)

BEST WOMEN IN the AIR.
BUT WILL IT ARRIVE?
BRITS WORST INVESTMENT
ANYWHERE.

C.A.A.C

(CHINA's only Airline until the'90s),
CARRIES ALL 'ANDBAGS CAREFULLY.

C.A.A
CIVILIAN AVIATION AUTHORITY
(BRITAIN)

CAMPAIGN AGAINST AVIATION.

DAN AIR
(as was)

Just had to be DAN DARE.

E.A.A.C EAST AFRICAN
(as was)

EVERY AFRICAN ALWAYS COMPLAINS.
EUROPEAN, AFRICAN & ASIAN CHKULA
(FOOD).

EMIRATES

EMI RATS.

GAMBIA AIRWAYS

Gambia STAIRWAYS.
It was a handling agent without any
aircraft.

GARUDA

When moved from Rangoon its base in
exile, to Jakarta, it was reconstituted &
partly, owned by K.L.M. It became known
by the unfair acronym:

4

GOES ALL RIGHT UNDER
DUTCH ADMINISTRATION.

GB Airways
(Gibraltar Airways)

Getting Better Airways.

GULFAIR

GOOF AIR.

J.A.L
(Japan)

JETS ALONG LAZILY
JOINS ALL LOINS.

KOREAN AIR LINES

KARATE AFTER LUNCH.

K.L.M

KINDLY LEAVE MONEY.

LAKER AIRWAYS
(as was)

SHAKER AIRWAYS.

L.O.T (POLISH)

LOADS OF TROUBLE.

LUFTHANSA
(GERMANY)

LET US F*** THE HOSTESSES AS
NO STEWARDS AVAILABLE.

M.A.S (MALAYSIAN)

MOST ASIANS SAIL.

M.E.A (LEBANON)

MONOTONOUS EXPERIENCE
ALWAYS.

NATIONAL AIRWAYS
(as was)

NEVER AGAIN.

NIGERIA AIRWAYS

No comic name, but they incredibly
use NIGAIR for their commercial
telex. Can you blame others?

NOVA AIR

Was B.C.A.L.'s Charter Arm which
had to change its name, it went for
NOVA AIR. Many wits, when asked
"Where are you going?" replied
"OH NO-VHERE".

PAN AMERICAN AIRWAYS
(as was)

Causes PANDEMONIUM AMONG
AIRLINES.

P.I.A
PAKISTAN
INTERNATIONAL AIRLINES

PLEASE INFORM ALLAH.

QANTAS-AUSTRALIA

QUEERS AND NANCY TYPES
AS STEWARDS.

QUENCH A NAGGING THIRST
AND SLUMBER.
QUAINT ASS.
Believe it or not, it derives from a
mouthful. An acronym of **Q**ueensland
And **N**orthern **T**erritory **A**ir **S**ervices.
Hence no 'U'.

SOUTH AFRICAN AIRWAYS SENSUOUS AIRBORNE AFFAIR.
SERVICE AN AFTERTHOUGHT.

S.A.S SEX AND SATISFACTION
SCANDINAVIAN AIRLINE SYSTEMS SEX AND SMORGASBORD.

S.A.B.E.N.A SUCH A BLOODY EXPERIENCE
(BELGIUM) NEVER AGAIN.
An even bigger mouthful than *QANTAS!*,
Societe **A**nonyme **B**elge d'**E**xploitation de
la **N**avigation **A**erinne.

S.I.A (Who would have insurmountable
SINGAPORE difficulties operating a domestic
INTERNATIONAL AIRLINES service!) SEEN IN ASIA.

T.A.P TAKE A PILL.
(PORTUGAL) TRY ANOTHER PLANE.

T.W.A TRY WALKING ACROSS.
TEENY WEENY AIRLINES, which after its
nineties massive route licence sales,
seems more appropriate.

UNITED AIRLINES LTD UNDRESS ALL LADIES.

UNITED ARAB AIRLINES UNDERSTANDING AS ALLAH.
(Egypt & Syria, as was)

U.T.A. (FRENCH INDEPENDENT) USUALLY, THEY'RE AROUND.
(As was)

VARIG VOLUPTUOUS AND ROMANTIC.
(BRAZIL) IN GENERAL. Like SABENA, an acronym of
Empressa de Viasa Aerae Rio Grandense.

VAYADOOT Translates to AIR Messenger. Many
(INDIAN domestic carrier) Indians call it VANYADOOT 'MESSENGER
of DEATH'.

ZAMBIA AIRWAYS   ZOMBIA AIRWAYS
(as was)

Etc,etc, if you know of any I have missed I would very much appreciate hearing from you, via **LONG ODDS LTD.,** P.O.Box 2132, Hove, East Sussex , UK, BN3 8AQ.

THE 21 YEAR OLD UNMIN

My secretary tried to get in and as usual, brief me on the problem. In spite of being a senior officer of the bank, my visitor brushed past her and in a raised voice abused me on British Caledonian's unaccompanied minors (UNMIN) initiative.

"Your claim to offer the best service is rot, my 14 year old daughter was left behind at Gatwick last night. We journeyed all the way to Lungi (Freetown Airport-a minimum of 6 hours round trip), arriving at 0600 this morning, only to find she was not on the flight".

He went on and on in an almost uncontrolled rage.

I must admit I was shaken. My company enjoyed a reputation second to none for the care of young **unaccompanied minors.** When, eventually, I was able to get a word in, I apologised and promised to try to call Gatwick (3,500 miles to the north).

Sadly, one could never be sure of getting a line, let alone getting through to the outside world. Having run into the anticipated line problems, I dispatched a 'QU' top priority non operational message. The then cost of this priority, was more than 400% the ordinary rate.

Within 30 minutes, Gatwick acknowledged my query adding that they had no record of an 'Unmin' having missed any flight the day before. They had found the passenger's name on the flight list but she had not checked in! Yes the passenger was listed as an 'Unmin', but as with other 'Unmins' who fail to turn up, they can only
a) Rely on the guardian advising parents.
b) Await the new booking.

They promised to make further enquires and revert as soon as possible. Having clearly got the strength of my irate parents' complaint across, I advised him of Gatwick's response and suggested he try to call the guardian.

Just after lunch, a second telex arrived on the subject. It was a real eye opener. I decided personally to take it to the bank officer in his office. On entering his office, all I said was "Before you say another word, I suggest that you read this" The telex read. 'We suffered a breakdown in the baggage belt operation when the subject passengers' flight was at 'Check In' Being the height of summer, this caused a backlog and we were calling passengers by both Public Address and Loud Hailers. We were confident that we had missed no one. Between 10 and 15 minutes after the flight had *taken off,* the Duty Officer was called to Check In. A gentleman presented a ticket on behalf of the young lady with him.

On discovering that it was for the subject flight, he told him that it had departed 10 minutes earlier. The gentleman complained about the back log. The young lady cut in with *"No problem, book me on the next flight"* (being Tuesday, the next flight was Friday morning). He asked the couple to go to the ticket desk.

With the Red & White striped UNMIN ticket cover warning sleeve removed, the Duty Officer did not notice the UNMIN code on the ticket.

However the Ticket Desk Agent did not miss it. He called the Duty Officer advising him that the ticket was that of a 14 year old UNMIN. He confirmed, that the appearance of the young lady, at least 21, totally bellied her actual age.

Even when confronted, she stated that her parents were aware of where she was and how she had missed the flight.
Not one colleague could believe, that she was only 14.

 # HIRED HANDS

An English airline captain on 'layover' in Sydney hailed a taxi.

The cabby, lowered the front passenger window with "Where to mate?" "Kings Cross", said the Englishman.

"Op in mate", said the cabby, opening the passenger door along side him. Instead, the captain opened the rear passenger door and got in.

"What's up wiv you mate?" the cabby enquired very sarcastically.

"I never ride alongside the hired hand" replied the captain.

"Pommy bastard", grunted the cabby.

DELTA- 'WE LOVE TO FLY & IT SHOWS'

Visiting Florida in January '91, we were driving north towards Orlando and listening to a local radio station in the vicinity of Fort Lauderdale.

The announcer was *pushing* a fete featuring Italy and those wonderful Italian foods.

The sponsor was DELTA Airlines whose 'sign off line' was

"WE LOVE TO FLY & IT SHOWS".

The announcer, keen to give their sponsor a 'plug', made a Freudian Slip. He said "The fete is sponsored by DELTA- 'WE LOVE **YOUR FLY** AND *IT SHOWS!"*

 # COMPLAINTS *FROM* THE STEWARDESSES

In a country in Africa, a European airline had an expatriate Commercial Manager well known for his amorous activities. Being in the tropics, he earned 42 days vacation per annum. He took 30 days in May.

On his return, he found the following *'pseudo'* memo written by his manager awaiting his return. Quote:

From Crewing Manager.   **STRICTLY CONFIDENTIAL**
To Commercial Manager XYZ.   **EYES of ADDRESSEE ONLY.**

CABIN STAFF MORALE.

Over the past few weeks, we have received a worrying number of complaints from female cabin staff about their 'layover' in XYZ.
Evidently, they find it becoming more and more frustrating.
Being personally aware of your amorous activities, I was hoping that you are either on vacation or are unwell. I trust that the former is the case and that

you will very soon be back on station and in action.

Should the latter be the case, I would strongly recommend that you discuss with your boss the problem, who will, I am confident, quickly come to the rescue of both the company, yourself and my staff.

Please let me know where we stand.

N.B. This memo is strictly for your eyes only.

Signed ....

The Commercial Manager was genuinely concerned that Crewing Manager should find it necessary to write to him in such terms.

THE 'DIP' COURIER

The international airline industry introduced Tourist Class back in the fifties. This changed the Free Baggage allowance and brought in many more passengers. The regulars were not happy. They wanted the exclusive use of First Class and 30 kilos but at the Tourist Class fares. The Round the World allowance dropped from 60 to 40 kilos, First Class remained at 30, while Tourist Class became 20 kilos International and 15 kilos on purely Domestic sectors.

Early one morning with B.E.A, when the changes were introduced, an American 'checked in' with a registered baggage weight of 34 kilos.

I explained that under the new regulations, he had 14 kilos in excess which had to be paid for.

The passenger protested vehemently adding, That except for what he had back home in Connecticut, this was all he had in the world. Not, as such, a very impressive statement. I diplomatically pointed out, that most people flying on commercial airlines were in the same position.

"But you do not understand, I was in the Le Bourget crash yesterday, I am entitled to 30 kilos. All my documents, passport, tickets etc, etc went up in flames" he pleaded as he apologised for his outburst.

The Le Bourget, crash I thought. A Convair 340 had 'gone in' a mere 12 to 14 hours earlier. Only about 10 out of 40 had survived and here was this fellow going back to Paris!

Further investigation revealed that he was a U.S. Diplomatic Courier. New documents had been issued in Paris and he came over on the last flight that night.

Naturally I allowed him the 30 kilo allowance 'losing' the other 4 kilos. I enquired of his attitude to taking another flight so soon after the crash and yet another a mere 14 hours later. "I've given up worrying about it" he calmly advised. Wide eyed, I asked "How come?"

"Well, you see, that was my sixth escape, as you know, I am a Dip Courier and I know nothing else. What's more the pay is very good".

'POMS'

When based in the antipodes, I had to make frequent visits to Australia where my Regional Head Quarters was located.

The majority of the visits were planned to coincide with the monthly marketing get together of the regional heads e.g. New Zealand, New South Wales, Queensland, Victoria, South Australia and Western Australia.

At some time, there would be a derogatory crack by one of the Australians about my being a 'Pom'. From day one, I chose to ignore or if I could, try to turn the crack into a joke at my own expense,

Frankly, it did me more good than harm. One day an Australian colleague, fed up with these childish cracks, chipped in with "For my money, Denis is very much a 'gruntled Pom'."

Fascinated, and ignorant of its meaning, I said, "Well I have been called many things in my life, but what on earth is a gruntled Pom?"

"Its the opposite to a disgruntled Pom", my supporter replied.

ETHNIC JOKES

Some of us, more than others, are the subject of having the rise taken out of us by another nationality or even a section of our own nationality.

One day in 1977 when I was B.C.A.L's G.M Advertising and Publicity, I was in Buenos Aires to give a talk on our plans for 1978 to a regional meeting of our South American colleagues .

Literally seconds after I started, our Sales Director was called to take an urgent telephone call from our Head Office in London. Anxious that he should also hear what I had to say, I stopped, explained my delay and awaited his return.

His absence became protracted and to hold the attention of my audience, I told a few of the stories found among these pages. A number refer to our lovely Irish colleagues, a nation with which I have strong maternal and paternal ties.

Having exhausted my immediate memory of anecdotes, I asked if any of those assembled would care to tell us a few stories. It became apparent, that it was a wide spread practice to 'take the mickey' out of other specific folk. I decided to do a small survey. The results are as follows.

THE TEASERS	THE TEASED
ENGLISH	THE IRISH.
LOWLAND SCOTS	HIGHLAND SCOTS who are called 'CHOOCHTERS' *(CHUCKTERS)*.
SWISS	THE GERMANS.
AUSTRIANS	THE GERMANS.
GERMANS	FRIESLANDERS.
CANADIANS	'NEWFOUIES'. NEWFOUNDLANDERS.
BRAZILIANS	THE PORTUGUESE.
PORTUGUESE	THE BRAZILIANS.
THOSE IN THE U.S.A	THE 'POLLACKS' POLES.
JAPANESE	KOREANS & CHINESE.
DANES	SWEDES.
NORWEGIANS	SWEDES.
RHODESIANS (ZIMBABWEANS)	'YARPIES' -SOUTH AFRICANS.
ENGLISH SOUTH AFRICANS	AFRIKAANS SOUTH AFRICANS.
AFRIKAANS SOUTH AFRICANS	RED NECKS- ENGLISH SOUTH AFRICANS.
KENYANS and UGANDANS	TANZANIANS.
MOST ARAB NATIONS	THE LEBANESE.
NEW ZEALANDERS	AUSTRALIANS and very much so,
AUSTRALIANS	NEW ZEALANDERS.
ARGENTINIANS	*ANY* SOUTH AMERICANS.
ITALIANS	SCILLIANS.

In fact, Italy is divided by the Po river. Those North vs those South of it and vice versa. The list is endless, with so much more within specific areas.

On a Mediterranean Cruise in 1975, we met a delightful American lady Travel Agent from Indianna who, after her return, persistently invited us to visit her & her family. With 5 days vacation available, we decided to go over for New Year.

Their extended family was very large and we were invited to join them at a New Year's Eve Dinner Dance to which we could bring Mark, then 10 years old. We said that we would prefer not to do so and would stay at home with him.

It was explained that with so many youngsters in the family, one of their parental couples stayed at home each year and cared for all the children. Mark joined them and we had a wonderful evening.

New Year's day was celebrated with a huge Bar-B-Q with all parents collecting their off spring. At the lunch, we were bombarded with complimentary remarks about our son and his wonderful sense of humour. It transpired that Mark decided to use his fund of 'Irish jokes'. Before doing so, he asked "Where does your family originate from, you know, Red Indians are original Americans?" "Oh we originate from Poland but were all born in the U.S.". To my horror, I could see it coming. Mark switched his Irish jokes to 'Polish' ones, we were about to become 'Persona Non Grata'. In the event our friends were wonderful, they thoroughly enjoyed him.

Oh I almost forgot, the Irish are as guilty as the rest of us. The butt of their humour are the 'Kerrymen', men from the county of Kerry.

My favourite ethnic joke is a visual but warrants telling i.e. it can be adopted to fit any others as you think fit.

'An Irish lad was in a pub which had a tropical fish tank about 36" x 18" x18" on the bar. A customer had his arm in the tank, with his fingers all set wide apart. With a glazed look, Paddy enquired of him "What are you doin?"

"I'm sending messages telepathically to the fish. Watch them slalom through my fingers".

Paddy, "Don't be bloody daft, yre havin me on, sure tha's rubbish"
"No, no be patient and watch. it is genuine" A fish slalomed through his fingers.

13

"Cmon, its a coincidence" said Paddy in disbelief.

"O.K, you select a fish and I'll prove it" said the mesmeriser. An apprehensive Paddy selected a distinctive white fish with black patches. After a few moments of intense concentration the selected fish performed. Paddy, still unconvinced, argued it was not possible.

The telepathist suggested "You tell me what would convince you".

Paddy thought deeply, "Tell them to reverse" he said with a wry smile.

"Boy you are tough, but I'll try" Minutes of intense concentration passed, eventually the selected fish slalomed backwards through the fingers. Paddy could not believe his eyes. "Sure tha's amazin, can any one do that?" he enquired. "Yes, if you concentrate hard and long enough" he was told. At that moment, the closing bell rang. Knowing the landlord, the regulars arranged for Paddy to be left in the closed bar (with a few beers) to practice.

At 1800, the regulars returned. Paddy was 'glued' to the tank base. The fish were not in the least interested in him. He had a deep glazed look of concentration, with his mouth opening and closing 'fish like'!

 # AND, AND, AND, AND, AND

The flight deck crew of a British Caledonian DC/10-30 en route Gatwick Los Angeles approximately an 11hr 30min flight, had invited a former East African captain travelling with them as a passenger to join them.

The guest asked if they ever got bored on these very long flights, when so much was through, relatively speaking, very quiet air highways. He said that on East Africans' overnight flights Nairobi - Europe, running about 7 to 8 hours, he often played word games with interested colleagues.

One challenge he had set remained after some months unsolved, would his hosts be interested?

"Why not, provided that you tell us the answer if we fail to come up with it", the B.C.A.L captain smiled.

"OK, give me a grammatically correct sentence, in which the word AND is repeated five times continuously. I assure you that it is possible said the guest.

Our crew thought for quite a long time before requesting the solution.

The explanation.

"A Publican was approached by an unemployed artist to repaint his badly weathered sign. The artist, hungry for work offered two rates. If the Publican was genuinely dissatisfied with the result, he would pay £30, if satisfied, the charge would be £50. The artist would rely on the Publican's integrity. The deal was struck.

When he had finished, the artist asked the Publican to inspect his work.

The Publican, an honest man, gave the artist £50 but added "While it is very good, I think that it would have looked much better if you had left more space between:

THE PIG **AND**, *AND,* **AND,** *AND,* **AND** THE WHISTLE".

Five times AND, grammatically correct.

'NUTS'

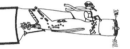

On a flight from Nairobi to Amsterdam, early in 1990, my wife and I were privileged to have our 'Up Grade' to First Class actioned. Soon after take off we were served drinks with small dishes of dry roasted nuts and canapes.

As time for dinner drew nigh a stewardess, who should have known better, when wishing to clear away our drinks and dishes said "May I pinch your nuts sir?" Realising her genuine 'faux pas', she turned scarlet and switched aisles with her colleague.

@@@@@@@@@@@@@@@@@@@@@@@@@@@@@@@@@@@@

Another lovely genuine 'faux pas' is credited to a stewardess who intercepted a passenger about to enter the toilet with a cigarette in his mouth. "Excuse me sir, smoking is not permitted in the toilets" she politely advised.

The passenger stubbed out the cigarette in the ashtray set into the toilet door. Since the passenger only wanted to adjust his clothing, he was out in seconds.

The stewardess, shocked to see him out so quickly said "If I had known you were going to be that quick, I would have been willing to hold it for you!"

LOTTERY ON THE NOSE-WHEEL

It is a little known fact by the general public, that U.K airlines are often highly committed to helping the underprivileged.

In British Caledonian, we formed the 'GOLDEN LION CHILDRENS' TRUST' which did sterling work under the chairmanship of the wonderful Harry Davies, honoured in 1994 by Esther Rantzen's *Hearts of Gold* Television Programme.

One of the numerous fund raising schemes, that help fund it, was that run by our air crews. Before take off, one of the flight deck crew, would chalk mark the number of crew members on their flight, clockwise onto the nose-wheel. He also made a mark on the wheel support.

The crew would then buy a raffle ticket, (taken out of a hat) at an agreed price bearing one of the numbers. Let's say £2. Fourteen crew realised £28, 60% would be allocated to the G.L.C.Trust with 40% being the prize for the ticket holder whose number was closest to the wheel support mark.

THE BALL

British Caledonian held a promotional evening in Kampala Uganda in 1971, followed by a cocktail party to which the 'layover crew' was invited.

Amongst our guests were members of the diplomatic service, who were potential customers. One guest, a French Diplomat 'took a shine' to one of our Air Hostesses. On hearing that she was on a 3 night 'layover' at Entebbe he invited her to be his companion at the forthcoming French Embassy Ball to celebrate the 14th July. On learning that it was an all evening dress occasion, she sadly declined the invitation.

Next day, poolside at the Lake Victoria Hotel Entebbe, she bemoaned her bad luck. All the more so, as the diplomat had offered to send his chauffeur to collect and take her back to Entebbe. A 19 miles each way journey.

The 'Purser' asked "What size are you?" and was pleased to hear confirmation that they were the same. "Right 'Cinderella', call your beau and ask him if the invitation is still open. I'll lend you the dress".

Our heroine, nervously called the Embassy posing the question. "Mais certainment my chauffeur will collect you at 1930 tonight, d'accord?" her beau responded.

The ball was a great success, equalled, according to many guests, by our heroine's evening dress. The guests eagerly enquired as to who designed such a gorgeous creation. Although sorely tempted, she explained that it was on loan.

'The dress' was a MARKS & SPENCER night dress.

Author modelling nightdress at charity ball 1962.

'LAS BREEZES' JEEP

A European major carrier used the same Advertising Agency as the famous 'Las Breezes' Hotel in Acapulco Mexico. A senior director of the Agency was on a visit to the carrier's Los Angeles office,

While there, he received a message telling him to urgently visit a potential new client A.S.A.P 'Down Town'.

His car would not start, the battery was flat and he went back into the office. He asked two staff, if he could borrow a car. One said "Willingly but its in for a service right now". the other said "Sure but I have a flat, if you change the wheel, the car is all yours". He said thanks but I simply do not have the time, I'll have to call a cab. Try though he may, it was in vain. The guy with the car with the flat said "Why did I not think of it before, take the jeep, its not required until tomorrow".

The jeep, in the pink and white stripes of the Las Breezes Hotel Acapulco (their property) , was in L.A in support of an advertising promotion the Ad Agents were organising. It had been parked behind the carrier's offices. The director was quickly away.

As he pulled up at a stop light, a guy in a coupé drew up alongside.

"A'int that a Las Breezes jeep?" he asked. "Sure is", said the director.

"How the hell did you get yer hands on that?" said the coupé driver.

"Some people steal coat hangers, some steal hotel towels" was the sharp response as he pulled away. He looked in his rear view mirror to see the coupé driver's reaction, as well as to ascertain what the cacophony of blaring horns was about. He saw the coupé driver's mouth wide open and all the cars behind him waving their arms gesticulating for him to move on.

PRIVATE MEDICAL

A Senior First Officer, who did not look after his health, knew that he might have difficulty in passing his next 6 monthly medical check due in 2 months. He decided to consult a private doctor.

Doctor . . . . .Do you smoke?
S.F.O . . . . .About two packs a week.
Doctor . . . . .Tens or twenties?
S.F.O . . . . .Two hundreds.
Doctor . . . . .Do you drink alcohol?
S.F.O . . . . .Two a day.
Doctor . . . . .Nips?
S.F.O . . . . .Bottles.
Doctor . . . . .Do you exercise regularly?
S.F.O . . . . .Now and again.
Doctor . . . . .Daily?
S.F.O . . . . .Yearly.
Doctor . . . . .Do you have sex?
S.F.O. . . . . .Infrequently.
Doctor *exasperated* . . .Tell me, is that one syllable or two?

THE RUGBY FORWARD

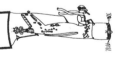

A number of airlines encourage their staff to form sports teams to compete with both other airlines and commercial house teams.

In B.C.A.L, we had cricket, rugby, netball, soccer etc, etc. I was president of the company Soccer Team 1975/76. We played numerous opponents and visited many overseas stations including KLM New York. They played under the auspices of Cosmos, the world famous New York club. Cosmos enjoyed the wonderful Pelé amongst its members.

Our rugby team was as active and I was told a story which the relator claims happened during one of their home 'internationals'. One of their Front Row Forwards, a huge bull of a man weighing in excess of 225 lbs, dislocated his right knee. He was carried off on a stretcher. The 'guest' club doctor went to attend to him because the team doctor had gone to the toilet. The 'guest' was very sympathetic.

However, when our doctor showed up, he agreed with the visitor, that the best solution was to manipulate the leg to try to get the joint back to normal.

The 'Forward' screamed his head off, the pain was so intense. The visiting doctor said that he thought the behaviour disgraceful, adding that only a couple of days earlier, he had delivered a woman of triplets and she did not make a fraction of the fuss the forward made.

"Great said the forward, I did not say a word when it came out. Try putting the bloody triplets back in and listen to the screaming she will provide!"

THE SCHOOL ESSAY

A colleague in British Caledonian was very keen to supervise his son's educational progress.

Each night, he would carefully check through the boy's homework after getting him to run-through the work done in class that day.

One evening, his son was telling about his first day in senior school and how his class had been told by their Head, that they were no longer children but adults.

To get his point home, the Head Master had instructed the English Tutor to set, as his homework, an essay on his talk.

The youngster then sat down to write the essay. His father would later 'vet' it but he would never correct it.

The work turned out to be most commendable and my colleague was quite impressed, that is, until he reached the final paragraph. It read, "I now look forward to the further pleasures of adultery!"

When our colleague told us about it, six of us in unison said "Like father, like son".

Being Scotland's national airline, British Caledonian made tremendous use of the 'Tartan'. The cabin staff had a selection of seven different tartans to choose from. I say choose, theoretically that was correct, however certain tartans were much more popular than others e.g. The Dress Black Watch. Since policy was for there to be a mix on every flight, Uniform Supplies had to restrict the freedom of choice.

Although not a Scot, I was always tremendously proud of our lassies and our image in general. We had one of very few airlines uniforms, which were so distinctive, that a B.C.A.L Air or Ground Hostess could be identified a very long way off. Two stories of the kilt warrant telling.

Probably the most asked question of a Scot wearing his kilt is:

"Is there anything worn under your kilt?" it comes from the belief, that 'The Ladies from hell,' the kilted Scottish regiments in war, never wore 'Y' fronts. The standard answer is "No madam, nothing is worn, everything is in perfect working order". A lass invited to check, exclaimed "Oh its gruesome. The Scot retorted, If you'd care to check again, y'll find it's grew some moore!"

Six Cale' lassies with author in Kampala 1971. Back row, extreme left is wearing Dress Black Watch Tartan.. One of these lovely lassies wore the M & S Nightdress in "THE BALL". Photo, Anne M. Long.

The second story follows naturally:

It was reported, that one of the broad Scots of B.C.A.L who attended the infamous 'Scottish Passenger Agents" annual Dinner became exceedingly drunk. On his way home, he realised that he was wandering all over the roadway. He decided to sit on the kerb, next to a lamp post for a spell. He fell soundly asleep. Two English girls, walking back to their hotel, saw 'Jock' they asked if he was O.K or if he needed any help. Jock, being out to the world, one girl said to the other, 'Now's our chance to find out if there really is anything worn underneath". They lifted his kilt and there, in all its glory, was his manhood. One of the girls, pulled a lovely red ribbon from her hair and gently, ever so gently, tied a bow around it.

Returning the kilt to its original position, they crept quietly away.The cold night wore on and Jock woke up somewhat more sober, he shook himself and walked on home.

As he entered his bedroom, he very quietly took off his jacket and set it over a chair back. He then did the same with his kilt but whilst trying to place it over the chair, he missed making a loud noise. Suddenly, all the lights came on. "Jock, is that you?" his frightened wife asked. "Aye indeed it is" said Jock. As she cleared her eyes, his wife went on "Where the hell have you been, do you realise that it is 5.30am?" Still the worse for wear, Jock swung around glancing a view of himself in the long wardrobe mirror. Confused he replied "Hell Morag, I can't remember but wherever it was, I won first prize!"

"I DID NOT HEAR ...."

On a beautiful sunny morning when I was seconded to Sierra Leone Airways, I was sitting poolside at the Bintumani Hotel Freetown, discussing the forthcoming days' activities with my (British Caledonian Airlines) U.K directors.

At that time, B.C.A.L "layover crews" used that hotel. Our First Officer joined our table for a chat.

A few minutes later, one of the female cabin crew members, a gorgeously shaped red head, strolled past. After a fleeting greeting of us, she said to the First Officer "I did not hear you get up". She carried straight on without turning her head, entering the restaurant for her breakfast.

The astonished First Officer, who had turned scarlet, expressed annoyance at both his unjustified display of embarrassment and the fact that he spent the night alone, in his own room one floor down from the lovely creature.

DUREX SPONSORSHIP

In charge of British Caledonian's U.K Field Sales based at Gatwick, I frequently travelled to and from London. Because of our long and close association with British Rail, we had a Barter-Trade Agreement. This provided B.C.A.L with invaluable First Class Rail Passes between Gatwick and the capital and British Rail with the equivalent value in travel on B.C.A.L.

The directors and Marketing Department held the passes because they had the greatest need and use of them.

One morning as I joined the 'Citylink' at Gatwick, a young businessman came into my compartment carrying a briefcase with a Formula One Racing Car sticker in a well known condom manufacturer livery sticker on the lid. He placed the briefcase in the overhead rack and read his newspaper. After 10 minutes, he took down the briefcase and started to work inside it. Fascinated, I asked my travelling companion "Is that sticker for real?" thinking it was a joke. "Indeed it is, have you not seen our cars or heard of it before?" he asked. "Why should I?" I said. "Where have you been these last few years, everyone knows of the controversy?"

"What controversy? I have been based in Africa and the South Pacific these past 12 years", I explained..

We sponsored a Formula One car but the 'Beeb' refused to televise races in which it competed, that is what the controversy was over.

"Be that as it may, I am staggered that such a promotion should be mounted at all, my having been B.C.A.L's General Manager Advertising & Promotions I know a thing or two about it". I went on.

The young man went to great pains justifying their decision. It was the ideal *vehicle* because of:
a) Today's promiscuous society.
b) His target 'A' and 'B' categories both male and female
   were tremendous supporters of Motor Racing.

"Great, I accept your advertising arguments but you have totally missed that element of the sport relative to your product" I reasoned.

"And what precisely is that?" he demanded sarcastically.
"What, I'll tell you what" said I. "What if your car has a puncture? "That's what!"

"My God! none of us have thought of that possibility". The very clearly worried young man exclaimed.

THE BENGALI

A dear old friend, Horace Hanson (R.I.P) was, many years ago, a Purser on Imperial Airways, (later B.O.A.C) Flying Boats.

For a number of years, he transited Calcutta, amongst all the other flying Boat stations. On the wall of the Calcutta Airport Manager's office hung the most magnificent Bengal Tiger skin. On each visit, Horace would, half jokingly offer to buy it. The A.P.M would impolitely tell him where to go.

One day, Horace 'landed' at Calcutta and the A.P.M greeted him with "Hanson, the very lad I have been looking for. I have had this lot, I have resigned. You have been on about the Bengali for so long, I have decided to make you a present of it".

Horace was over the moon and in the same breath, he invited the A.P.M out to dinner and in instructed the 'bearer' to wrap it in a cardboard box and have it ready for his departure next day.

Just after take off next morning, Horace was anxious to look at his prize possession. As he opened the box, the captain came down from the upper deck (The 'Boats' were similar to today's 747s, in that the flight deck was on an upper level from the main passenger deck). "What have you there?" enquired the captain. "Just a second skipper, wait until you see this", Horace proudly replied, taking the string off the box. He put his hand inside to pull the skin out but all he got was a handful of fur. Horace was crest-fallen. "What can I do." skipper he pleaded. "Nothing, absolutely nothing. There is no way that you can stick each and every one of those hairs back in. Best thing, is to get rid of it now".

With that, the captain opened a port hole (no pressurisation in those far off days) and pushed the skin out.

A steward, back in the cabin was taking drinks orders. As he approached an

23

elderly retired Colonel of the Indian Army, the old man said with a hiccup "I know that I may already be pissed, but I am certain I just saw a Tiger run past our aircraft!"

REMEMBER WHERE YOU ARE

I understand that there was terrific rivalry between the Flying Boat and the Land Plane aircraft crews of Imperial Airways and B.O.A.C.

A flying boat pilot, was in need of a flight check after having been off sick for a number of weeks. Due to operational demands and the need to get the pilot back on line, a land plane 'Check Pilot' was assigned to the task.

Prior to and immediately after the 'check', he ribbed the Flying Boat pilots on the superiority of Landplane pilots.

On disembarking from the 'boat', still talking to and looking at the crew following him to the exit, the 'Check Skipper' stepped out straight into the water!

HIJACK

As a delegation member to the I.A.T.A Conference in Dakar, Senegal on Airport Security in 1978, I witnessed a very heated argument principally between, representatives of the pilots associations on the one hand and airport commandants and their staff on the other.

The basis of disagreement, was that the ground authorities, most not all, wanted to close their airports to hijacked aircraft. To do this, they would place full oil barrels strategically along the runway.

The pilots, quite reasonably argued that as this was pushing the problem to another airport it was irresponsible and prolonging the agony of those in the aircraft. The aircraft could not stay indefinitely in the air! They argued very forcefully for a favourable decision. As the discussion progressed it became more acrimonious.

A friend, was conference chairman. He had a very difficult situation on his hands, I pressed the button on the 'mic' in front of me, indicating to the chairman, that I wished to speak. When invited to do so I advised that we

24

should follow the measure adopted by Eastern Airlines after suffering a series of hijackings.

They asked their staff to suggest action. One wit wrote in suggesting, that just before departure of all flights destined for Miami, we play the Cuban National Anthem and arrest all who stand up!

DECORUM

Most of the B707 crew on 'layover' at the Airport Motel were sitting around an oblong table enjoying a mid afternoon drink. A junior hostess and a steward came from the pool in their swim wear and joined their colleagues. The girl sat at the far end of the table and rested her right ankle on her left knee. The unsightly view of a large quantity of pubic hair was observed by her male colleagues at the other end. One, the captain, suggested that she should keep both her feet on the ground.

In a haughty voice, the girl said " I will sit exactly as I please". The captain in a very controlled polite voice replied "Very well, if nothing else, it keeps all the flies down your end".

The girl, furious and scarlet with embarrassment, stormed off to her room to the applause of the rest of her crew.

 # THE DOG DERBY

The Irish are well known for their love of racing. In the early fifties, they had an excellent chance of winning THE DOG DERBY (championship greyhound race) run in England.

Their champion, was in the Freight Shed at Collinstown airport Dublin. Most of the staff had money on the dog, some a great deal. They persuaded the Exports Manager to bring out the animal for them all to admire. Now Collinstown Airport was very much a country airport. While all were showering compliments and praise on the dog, no one, no one that is save the dog, noticed a hare appear on the grass verge a few yards away. In a flash the greyhound had wriggled out of his halter and was off at a tremendous pace after the hare. The chase was on. The dog in full flight after the hare, all his admirers in full flight after the dog. After all, they were the cause of this dreadful situation.

The search, to no avail, carried on for hours.

Eventually, someone had to go to the V.I.P Lounge, where they found the dog in one of the armchairs almost exhausted, his tongue almost touching the floor. Panic, the dog was running that night. It was given a very strong dose of brandy. Unfortunately, the animal came in last, to the bewilderment of all, except those employed at Dublin Airport who had admired their hero earlier in the day.

THE MYSTERIOUS TRUNK

In British European Airways Waterloo Air Terminal (circa 1954), we engaged retired airport coach drivers to run our Left Luggage Office.

Break relief was always provided by the Interline and Arrivals Section close at hand. One afternoon when I was in charge of the desk, we were short handed and I undertook the Left Luggage relief. Two gentlemen came to the counter and one handed me a receipt marked FLOOR, the location of the baggage. Neither gentlemen spoke, other than to pass the time of day. I searched the rear of the store but found nothing. I asked the gentleman who gave me the receipt for a description, in case it had been moved. Not an uncommon action between the men who normally worked there. They always briefed each other like aircraft commanders at hand over. "You cannot possibly miss it, it is a very large black trunk" he sarcastically advised me.

No wonder the receipt had FLOOR written on it. The claimant added "However, it is not very heavy, since it is almost empty". As I returned to the rear of the store, I knew that it was not there but went through the motions. Returning, I advised the gentlemen that it was not there.

"Perhaps a friend or relative had collected it against a Form of Indemnity. (Used when documents were lost). "Definitely not, you had better give me your Indemnity Form" he demanded.

"I am afraid that will not do as you will need to submit a claim supported by your receipt sir", I explained. Unlike a lost piece of registered baggage, we had no way of tracing it. Further, it was not the sort of thing someone might take by mistake.

The gentleman, not at all happy at his having brought a van to collect the trunk, took the receipt and left quite annoyed. None of us could guess what had happened. About three weeks later, the claim was processed and compensation paid. Two or three weeks later still, we received a telex message from Dorval Airport Montreal. It read:

HOLD A LARGE SEA GOING TRUNK- ONLY IDENTIFICATION IS A B.E.A WATERLOO A/T LEFT LUGGAGE LABEL- PLEASE ADVISE.

We replied by urgent message:

THIS MYSTERIOUSLY GONE MISSING FROM OUR LEFT LUGGAGE GRATEFUL IF YOU WOULD RETURN IT ASAP BY SERVICE CARGO e.g. F.O.C.

The next telex from Dorval caused even more confusion:
REGRET ADVISE TRUNK WILL NOT FIT INTO HOLD OF ANY AIRCRAFT CURRENTLY SERVING DORVAL IF YOU WISH WILL INVESTIGATE COSTS OF RETURNING BY SEA ON CHARGES COLLECT BASIS OR COULD HOLD ON UNTIL UNSCHEDULED ALL CARGO FLIGHT DESTINED LONDON APPEARS. ADVISE!

THE BIRTHDAY PRESENT

A captain of the Jewish faith and his wife lost all the sparkle in their love life. To spice things up, a psychologist counselled that the captain pay his wife for her favours. It worked a treat and the months passed happily by.

One morning, there was a loud motor horn blasting away outside their house. The captain got out of bed and went over to the window. In the drive he saw a brand new Jaguar saloon with the very latest registration. "Rachel, Rachel, who the hell do we know with a brand new Jag' that would call on us this early on Saturday, quick, quick come and see".

Rachel laying in bed said "We don't know anyone, it's your birthday present" "My what?" "I told you once, its your birthday present from me" "Where the hell did you get enough money for such an expensive gift?" he demanded.

"Well, you know all that money you have been giving me every time we make love,"

"Yes, yes" he excitedly queried.

"Well I saved, *et voila,* your birthday gift" "Good God Rachel, what a wonderfully thrifty woman you are". Thoroughly overcome he momentarily forgot himself "If only I had known what you were up to, I would have given you *all* my business"

27

Photo courtesy of Jerry Rycroft collection.

Until he was 21, my son Mark enjoyed the use of my rebated travel privilege. Because of his very close association with my colleagues in B.C.A.L, he made a number of friends there. One of his closest friends was a junior member of Cabin staff, who would invite Mark to secure an ID90% rebate ticket over the route he was scheduled to operate.

Mark could stand by for his flights, safe in the knowledge that he would be given a crew rest seat and not be left behind in the event of a flight being full. Cabin staff are allowed to permit a friend or relative use their rest seat because they can vacate it when required by operational staff..

On the occasion in question, Mark's friend was going to Hong Kong via Dubai. On both outward and return journeys, two night's rest were allocated at each point, where Mark could use his friend's room, his friend would share his girlfriend room, she being on the crew. Mark already knew well, two of the three pilots and a fair number of the cabin staff. The Flight Deck Crew consisted of the Captain, First Officer, a 'Check Captain' and a very senior Captain who was checking the Check Captain. They all got on like a family and many pranks were played on the Flight deck Crew at both Dubai and Hong Kong with Mark in the thick of it.

The captains resolved to get even with Mark at the second Dubai 'layover'. They suggested playing LANCASTER BOMBERS, an old R.A.F bit of fun.

The idea is, for 13 players to sit in a formation laid out as a 'Lanc' i.e:

			No 4 Engine	
			No 3 Engine	
Co Pilot	**Flt Engineer**		
'NOSE'				**'TAIL'**
Nose Gunner		**Mid Upper Gunner**	
Bomb Aimer/Observer	**Navigator**		**Rear (Tail) Gunner**
Pilot	**Radio Operator**	
		No 2 Engine	
		No 1 Engine	

The pilot would give orders with his fingers pinching his nose to sound like the aircraft radio. When he would say "start No 1", the person sitting in that position was required to make a noise like an old style engine coughing and spluttering into life. They were also required to rotate their arm like a propeller. Orders with appropriate actions would continue through the 'flight'. Mark was given the No 4 Engine position. The set up was, for the Pilot to declare a fire in No 4 engine. The female purser of their real crew, was primed to come out of the bathroom on hearing the *FIRE* call, and empty an ice bucket of very cold water over Mark.

After a reasonable period of flight, the pilot said *FIRE* in No 4, *FIRE* in No 4. Mark made the appropriate noises e.g. coughing and hissing. The *FIRE BRIGADE* emerged from the bathroom behind Mark. In her excitement, she became confused and emptied the freezing water all over No 1 Engine position. All agreed, it was yet another example of a female not knowing her Left from her Right.

DAMAGED PRIDE

The Sierra Leone Airways Trilander 9L-LAU, at Hastings, Freetown's domestic airport, was fuelled to the gunwales ready for its next up country flight.

Across, on the far side of the Ramp, a Cessna182 had been parked. Its German pilot had been evaluating a student pilot who it was claimed, had been trained to fly helicopters in China. The German was not impressed with his charge who was temporarily employed as a General Duties clerk in the Charter company's office.

The student, whose head was already very swollen with his own ideas of his future, was boasting to a cleaner. He invited the cleaner to accompany him over to the Cessna where he would demonstrate his knowledge. The keys to the aircraft hung on a hook in the office, it was no problem for the 'student' to access them. Once in the aircraft, the student fired her up. Unfortunately, the German had forgotten to 'chock' the wheels and the 182 lurched forward.

Panic struck the 'student' who pushed home the throttle causing the aircraft to race across the Tarmac ramming straight into the waiting Trislander. Amazingly, in spite of the highly volatile Avgas and 13 deep cuts into the wing of the Trislander, it neither caught fire nor did it explode. Yet another incredible thing was the delay sustained by the Trislander. On the morning circuit from Freetown to Bo, Kenama and Yengama and back the same way, it sustained a rare puncture. Changing the wheel causing the delay. Had the 1400 operation been on time, there is no doubt that there would have been an horrendous accident.

Cessna 182 rammed into Trislander. Note cuts in Trislander wing. Photo, author.

After the accident, it was decided, that repair of the Trislander in Sierra Leone, was beyond economic reasoning. I therefore, had to vet a replacement aircraft evaluated by B.C.A.L on S.L.A's behalf. One possibility, was in the lovely Channel Island of Jersey.

My day visit, coincided with the celebration of the WWII 'Battle of Britain'. On my way back to London, I was well ahead of the scheduled reporting time. Invited out onto the Tarmac, I was watching the wonderful variety of WWII aircraft doing 'low level wheels up' runs over a runway, prior to their landings, after their ceremonial flight over St. Helier.

Very close by, was a WWII ex- Squadron Leader of the R.A.F, typical of his type, full of his own importance he said to me "Thar mi lad, what d'ya think o' that?" as a magnificent Lancaster Bomber flew past.

"Superb", I replied

"Makes ya heart thump", he went on.

The 'Lanc' landed and taxied to a halt not 60' away from us. The Squadron Leader drooled on.

One by one, the crew descended from the ladder a midships, eventually the Captain appeared, the squadron Leader expressing his envy.

As *SHE* removed *HER* flying helmet, it was abundantly clear, that the Squadron leader was shell shocked.

His disgust was very clear, his words unprintable.

'YOUR PLOOF'

When B.C.A.L introduced its daily service to Hong Kong, it employed Chinese speaking Stewardesses and Passenger Service Agents. One evening a 'pretty couple' had considerable excess baggage which they paid for without argument. Whilst the Passenger Services Agent wrote out their receipt, the conference facility on her desk, came to life. She pressed the answer button and spoke to 'control'.

The query was heard throughout all 'Check In' Desks. When finished, she forgot to switch off. As she handed the documents back to the passengers, she referred to each one: "Here are your tickets, Baggage Claim Tags for you. five legistered baggage are attached to your ticket cover. These are your Bloading Passes with the arrocated seat numbers and this is your ploof."

"Our what?" the passengers angrily asked.

"Your ploof, your ploof" she said, with the customary problem that most Chinese have with 'Rs' & 'Ls'.

The indignant passengers, hearing her voice coming out from the adjoining desks, said, "We know that we are gay, but it is not your place to broadcast it all over the terminal!"

"DOST STILL REFUSE TO PAY THY EXCESS BAGGAGE CHARGES?"

IDD il FITTRE

The Line Station's Superintendent came to one of three stations he was to visit for his Engineering Checks. He arrived Friday evening, planning to cover the other two on his way home. Saturday morning in the Area Manager's office, he handed in a note of his planned itinerary for his visit to all three stations.

He was surprised and very annoyed to hear, that the New Moon was expected that night or latest Sunday night which would announce Idd il Fittre the end of the Holy Month of Ramadan. The Muslims' Easter. When announced, it would bring in a two day holiday. All locals celebrated both Christian and Muslim holidays. On Monday and Tuesday therefore, there would only be a skeleton staff on duty in the Engineering Department.

The visitor was searching for someone to blame for his potential waste of time. In his anger he said, "I do not need to fly 3,500 odd miles to see a bunch of 'idle fitters', I have more than I need at home".

THE UNEXPECTED FLIGHT

A BAC 1-11 was undergoing high speed braking tests at Gatwick. As the aircraft sped along the runway, literally seconds before the brakes were about to be applied, the aircraft lifted off.

'So what', you might ask. So what indeed. The aircraft was airborne with all the 'pins' in. The 'pins' are inserted at strategic points such as hydraulic landing gear and in flight control units, to prevent them from being inadvertently activated when the aircraft is on the ground e.g. raising the undercarriage which would cause considerable and expensive damage. However, airborne the aircraft was deprived of essential controls. The shortage of fuel speaks for itself, however it had yet another problem, the aircraft had not been subjected to the essential 'weight and balance' disciplines.

Mercifully, on board was one of B.C.A.L's most experienced captains, who skillfully brought the 1-11 safely back to earth. To the considerable relief of all of those on board, A.T.C, the Fire Brigade, Ambulance Services, the company and by no means least of all the technical crews' families. (See front cover)

There is no doubt, that some people have a knack with animals where others do not. The knack has different levels, some can handle very angry creatures, whereas others cannot get on with normal animals. Some folk who hate animals, attract them!

One day, a rather unsocial dog arrived at Heathrow Cargo Unit London and the duty staff repeatedly called the consignee throughout the day without response. Concerned, they tried to give it morsels of meat obtained from the canteen. Its growls and snarling teeth were rather off putting. The staff were not dismayed, a colleague due on at 1400, was known to have that mysterious gift.

When he signed on, he was taken straight to the crate in which the dog was housed. A clear attitude improvement was noticed when the new man approached the dog, it accepted the food he offered.

More futile attempts were made to contact the consignee. The man with the ability to reach out to the dog, decided to bring in a choker chain next day to exercise the animal, if it had not been collected. At 2200, just before going off duty, he fed the dog.

Next day, the same story, no response from the consignee. the Duty Officer resolved to telex the originating station for disposal instructions. When our hero came on at 1400, next day, he carefully opened the cage door, slid he choker chain over the dog's head and took him for a walk around the airport. Putting it back into the cage was no problem at all, our man becoming attached to the dog, prevailed on his boss to wait another 24 hours before sending 'his request for disposal' instructions.

Next afternoon, the feeding and walk went off without incident.

At about 1630 a gentleman walked into 'Imports' full of apologies. "I was on my way home from a skiing holiday when an avalanche came down and cut off the road. When I eventually reached home I found your Arrival Advice Note. Before even unpacking, I got straight into my station wagon and drove here. May I please collect my Siberian Wolf?" before he could continue, the 'Imports Clerk' said "We do not have a Wolf sir".

"Oh yes you do, and I wish to pay whatever additional charges are outstanding". The Clerk went cold, Wolf, Wolf, he croaked "May I see your Air Way-bill please sir?" The number tallied with that on the 'dog's' cage.

NASA and THE SHUTTLE

The aircraft was still at the Gate some 27 minutes after scheduled departure, with no sign of an immediate movement, the captain switched on his Public Address. "Ladies and Gentlemen, your Captain. A short time ago, NASA brought back its latest Space Shuttle, 1 minute 15 seconds late after travelling some 1.767,000 miles. Here we are, about to undertake a journey not 500 miles from London and yet this lot just cannot get their act together".

SICK SOLDIER

At Ciampino airport Rome circa 1952, we had 2 delayed aircraft a B.E.A Viking and a B.O.A.C Argonaut, plus a S.A.A 'Connie' on time in transit. A QANTAS 'Connie' was due to transit quite soon. We were s-t-r-e-t-c-h-e-d.

The Qantas Connie, had radioed that they had, as expected, a terminally sick soldier on board. A Brit, he was en route from Singapore to London.

When Qantas landed, I went up the front steps to be greeted by the biggest steward I have ever seen. He almost filled the doorway. "Wacha bluie, which do ya want first, the dead 'uns or the live 'uns?"

"You lost the soldier then" I suggested.
"Yeah he died" advised the smiling Steward.
"I know, I know, just after the point of no return" I quipped sarcastically.
"That's right, how did you guess?'" he replied with a broad grin.

In those days, if a death occurred on board, before the aircraft was half way to its destination, they were supposed to turn around and go back to the last departure point. A crazy rule much abused for very sensible reasons.

"Right, get the live ones off first" I requested. Being pushed, I left the Cabin & Ground staff to their duties. When I returned to the aircraft, the incoming crew had vanished. I had forgotten that they were due to 'layover' at Rome. Being there on relief. I called the Loaders from under the aircraft asking them to help me carry the body across the tarmac. "Signore, we 'andle alla types of

35

cargo but a nota toucha deada cargo. Scusi". As the loaders descended the steps, the joining captain came aboard. His transport had been delayed and the 'hand over' had taken place in the Briefing Room.

"What's your E.T.D (Estimate Time of Departure) he asked.

"That, is entirely dependant on you. You have a corpse on board, the loaders will not touch it, I cannot get it off on my own and unless you are prepared to take it on to London, you will have to help me carry it off. Otherwise you are going nowhere". The Captain took off his jacket, removed his epaulettes from his shirt and said "O.K what do we do?" I suggested that we uncover the soldier's face and carry him on a stretcher if he was asleep. It would attract much less attention.

PROBLEM, where the hell are we going to put him?

We had an old B.E.A coach (the type I called 'the half double decker') All the seats had been gutted and the interior turned into an Operations Office. The body would have to be laid on the floor. We felt bad about it, dashing in and out but with

'the half double decker'

kilometres of paper work required to 'land a body', it would have to await the departure of all the current batch of aircraft.

IF YOU PLAN ....'

As a young Traffic Assistant with B.E.A at Northolt Airport (London) circa 1950, I was on the late shift awaiting the arrival of a delayed DC3 from Belfast.

When the aircraft was about an hour out, the skipper radioed that he required a doctor to meet him, he had a very sick passenger on board.

We called the stand by because the duty man was himself off sick.

The 'DAK' landed, we were all on the ramp anxious to clear it. The Duty Officer disembarked the walking passengers and we filed on behind the doctor.

When he had examined the patient, the doctor pronounced him dead. "My

God, I spoke to him not 20 minutes ago", said the Captain.. "That is incredible, I reckon he has been dead for over an hour", the doctor said as he walked down the central and only aisle. The doctor had forgotten his bag and was going to collect it. I turned to the Captain and said. "But Captain, when you spoke to the passenger, he did not answer, did he?"

The Captain, while focussing a most penetrative stare said "Young man, *if you plan* a career in aviation, you will keep your mouth firmly shut".

THE HEART FOUNDATION

British Caledonian was approached by the British Heart Foundation to see if any of its Captains would agree to be 'wired up' to monitor their stress levels. One Captain agreed to the test, was well known for his cooperative attitude.

The Foundation believed that the E.C.G would register varying degrees of stress at:
  a) Push back.
  b) Engine start up.
  c) Break release.
  d) On Take Off   i) Run – climaxing with   ii) Lift Off.
  e) At start of decent.
  f) Entering the Ground Approach Control Zone
  g) Joining 'Long Finals' Through the last 250' to the runway, climaxing seconds before actual touch down.

When the reading was checked, the line was perfectly straight throughout. Clearly the machine was faulty. "Would the Captain be willing to 'suffer' the slight discomfort again?" He most certainly would.

The result was the same. this captain did not react badly to stress. He took everything in his stride. But there again, those of us who worked with him, did not need any E.C.G test to tell them that.

A VERY FUNNY LEBANESE

A Lebanese Christian on an African station, was renowned for his wonderful sense of humour and mimicry.

One afternoon, he called at the surgery of his friend and mine, a super Gynaecologist who cared for our wives.

When shown into the surgery, the Lebanese gruffly threw the Gynaecologist's account onto his desk with "Just what is this all about?"

Even though well used to his visitor's pranks, he was a little taken a back.

"It is my account", said the doctor. "You cannot have forgotten that I attended your wife throughout her recent confinement and delivery".

"You, you, for the past nine months, twice a week, you have had my wifes' knickers off and now, you have the effrontery to bill me for the pleasure".

With that, he exited before his friend could say another word.

THE DEPARTURE TAX

A Sinhalese family of 7 were at Freetown airport about to join a B.C.A.L DC10 service to Gatwick en route to Dubai. At the Departure Tax booth, the father had only sufficient U.S.$ to pay for 6, he asked if he could pay the small balance of $5 equivalent in local currency. It was only 7% of the total charge.
The official said a firm "NO".
"But I simply could not buy any more dollars. let me pay at the black market rate" he pleaded. "NO" the official would not give.

"I'll pay one and a half times the black market rate" The father pleaded further. "NO" they stood firm. "What on earth am I supposed to do then, it is your government that is unable to make dollars available?" With the utmost sincerity, the official said "Leave your baby behind!!"

The father was devastated at such a suggestion. In tears he explained his plight to my Airport Manager who resolved the problem by paying the $5 from his own pocket. With our next flight some 3 days off, we could not afford to lose a family of 7 all the way to Dubai for the sake of a lousy $5.

THE TEXAN

In the days of DC4 transatlantic air travel, a Texan on whose land oil in vast quantities had been found, decided to visit Europe. He was very green indeed, having never been outside his little town in Texas, let alone outside his country.

On the DC4, he was fascinated to see a film starlet smoking a cigarette in an extremely long holder.. He went over to the young lady. "S'cuse me maam, ahmm a Texan going to Europe for the furst taime. Whats thart thin you got yrr cigarette in?

"It is a nicotine preventative" she replied.

"Ah what?" he retorted "What the hell is thaat furr?"

"It keeps the brown stuff off your fingers" she said showing him how clean hers were.

"Does everyone in liddle ol England use one?"

"Everyone who is anyone does" she advised

"What do yerr call it again maam?"

"A nicotine preventative, nicotine preventative. Got it?

"Where do I git one? he eagerly enquired."Oh any drug store, just tell them which cigarette you smoke, you know Philip Morris, Chesterfield whatever and they will give you the correct size"

The Texan returned to his seat and slept. In the morning, he was again asking the starlet what the darned thing was called. "A *nicotine* preventative, *nicotine* preventative, a *nicotine* preventative, keep saying it over and over.

In customs, the Texan again asked, what the holder was called. She reiterated. In baggage reclaim he went to her yet again. Sorry maam, but what that darned thin called."

"A NICOTINE PREVENTATIVE, say it , (he did) now go straight around the corner to the drug store, I'll watch you bags".

The Texan ran to the chemist where he found a lovely tall blond smiling and happy to help. "May I help you sir".

"Yeah, I wanna, wanna, gor dam it, oh yeah, I wanna preventative".

"Fine sir, what size would that be?"

To fit a CAMEL" he replied.

The blond fainted!

TEE FLAGS

We (B.C.A.L), were already involved in the Sierra Leone 'OPEN' Golf Tournament but were approached by the organisers to pick up the costs of a new set of 18 Tees. Evidently the original sponsor had gone bust.

Our advertising budget was able to cope but with only 8 days to the start, I insisted on a clause in the contract 'if the tee flags are not delivered by 0800 hours on a given date, then we would not be required to pay for them'. To ensure that the Flags were exactly as we required them, clearly showing our logo, we made up a full size 'mock' Tee Flag for the manufacturer to work from.

On the morning of the start of the competition, 0800 arrived but no Tee Flags. The Club was annoyed. We were disappointed but financially safe. The club secretary produced the old worn and tattered flags for distribution to all 18 holes. As the Green Keeper was about to set off, a van screeched into the parking lot. The driver explained that, there had been a major accident blocking the road, borne out by other late arrivals. The Tee Flags were proudly presented in their opened box.. They looked superb, exactly conforming to the design provided. Problem was, they had, all 18 of them, the same No1!!

THE SEXY SALES PROMOTION

In Uganda, every six weeks, I would do a marketing circuit of the Safari Lodges and Copper Mines located up country. I would maintain contact with the lodge management, tour operators and couriers often in a position to either, keep a group with your airline in the event of a delay or conversely, bring a group to ones carrier in the event of another carrier's delay. Finally, I kept in touch with the Mines personnel Managers who indulged in both duty travel and some personal travel. They also permitted me to leave promotional material in support of both types in their offices.

My predecessors had set up a unique 'Sexy Sales Promotion' gimmick in one of the mine social clubs. He secured a genuine pair of air hostess panties which he had mounted on a wooden shield. This was competed for by the social clubs Darts Teams.

It was quite strange how much interest this generated amongst the female members. The males we expected to play hard for it, but the females, now they were an added bonus.

THE LOST GREEK

A prominent member of the local Greek community had died at an African station of Alitalia and considerable competition ensued to get the family to use a given airline to

a) get the body back to Athens(excellent Cargo Revenue) and

b) carry the six or seven family members Round Trip First Class who would accompany it. Marco worked very hard and won on the strength of his promising to personally supervise the loading of 'Papa' in spite of the monsoon rains. Marco bought a 'Sou' wester' outfit, wellies and stout rubber gloves.

Good to his word, he was on the tarmac near the aircraft hold, directly underneath the First class cabin to oversee the loading of the coffin.

From the indications in the cabin, the family were well pleased and grateful. Their gratitude very soon disappeared when in Athens, as the coffin was nowhere to be found. In fact Fiumicino (Rome Airport) had already advised the originating station a few hours earlier with a copy to Athens that it did not arrive.

In the certain knowledge that the coffin had left base, Marco was confident that it had been off loaded at a transit call en route to Rome. Confident that the problem lay there, he still called Rome cargo to make absolutely certain it had not been mishandled there. Rome were adamant, 'NOT RECEIVED'.

He then called his Capo Scalo (A.P.M) 'up the line' he too was adamant that he had not requested *anything* off loaded. Some mystery, but it had to be somewhere. Marco decided to go to next door neighbours, he had to do something. He knew that he trusted his *friend* running 'next door' but what else could he do?

As he was about to leave for his visit, his office called to advise 'The family are leaving Athens for their African home via Rome in First class, at Alitalia's expense. At the transit station, the A.P.M took Marco through both freight sheds, incoming and outgoing. Sure enough, no coffin was there.

The A.P.M' secretary then advised that the Greek Ambassador was on his way to the airport to talk to them. "What the hell are we going to say to the man?

"A coffin cannot simply disappear into thin air, or can't it" said the A.P.M

"Then where the hell is it, I saw it leave my station, you assure me that you did not request its off load here, and it has not, according to Rome arrived there?" demanded Marco as they subconsciously drifted away from the terminal and out across the Ramp. With literally nothing more to say on the subject, they started to discuss yesterday's Italian soccer results in Italy.

Suddenly the A.P.M noticed a large box on a trolley way out past the West Passenger Loading Pier. They quickened their step in spite of the burning sun.

As they neared the trolley they said, "it has to be the coffin". On arrival, they located the Cargo label which to their relief, confirmed their thoughts.

The A.P.M noticed that the local airline's service due to depart to London via Rome was still on the Ramp. He ran like the wind, wringing wet with perspiration to find the Duty Manager who could authorise the holding of the aircraft.

With the coffin safely on board, the pair remained on the Ramp to see it airborne. Having seen it away, they called Rome instructing no one less than the Cargo Manager to meet the aircraft supervise the transfer to the first available flight to Athens. he was required to also intercept the family and assure them that 'Papa' would be with them shortly.

Investigation subsequently revealed that, when the Alitalia DC8 transited, the loaders had a very bulky large item of cargo. To get it on board, they decided to off load the large box in transit. Subsequently, local carrier denied all responsibility for the problem, claiming that the Alitalia A.P.M was responsible. They steadfastly refused to accept, that he could not alone lift the coffin weighing in excess of 250 kilos+ on his own.

'IS A NOT MIA LUIGI!'

Three Italians died at the same time, in different parts of the Eastern U.S.A, by coincidence, their remains were to fly on the same aircraft JFK- Rome.

All three coffins, were delivered to Export Cargo JFK at approximately the same time. When the Air Waybills were cut, the Cargo clerk got the labels mixed up. Transfer at Rome was smooth and efficient. The coffins were at their destinations early afternoon on the day of their arrival in Italy. Funeral arrangements were running well, until one distraught mother living in Rome, insisted on saying farewell to her beloved Luigi.

Against all advice, she insisted on the coffin being opened. There was the most awful scream followed by "IS A NOT MIA LUIGI".

It was not, and to make things worse both of the other coffins had to be exhumed to establish which was Luigi. Think about it, this could not have been easy with the other cemeteries being in, Milano and Palermo!

RIGHT & LEFT HAND

It was decided to standardise driving practice throughout West Africa. Previously, the Francophile countries had left hand drive, while the Anglophiles had right hand drive. A presidential decree was issued in one Anglophile state: It read

**"TO MAKE EASY THE INTRODUCTION
OF THE CHANGE TO**

LEFT HAND DRIVE.

PLEASE NOTE VERY CAREFULLY.

TRUCKS, BUSES and HANDCARTS

WILL CHANGE OVER BETWEEN THE

1st. AND THE 10th OF NEXT MONTH

ALL OTHER VEHICLES WILL CHANGE

OVER FROM THE 11TH.

Oh really?

 # THE GREEN STEWARDESS

When based in Zambia, I visited Lusaka or Salisbury (now Harare) at least twice a month. I got to know the stewardesses of Central African Airways quite well. Although 'Free Seating' was C.A.A's official policy, the girls always kept a seat for me in the last row of the Viscount.

On one trip to Salisbury, as soon as the continental breakfast had been cleared away. As she winked at me from behind the junior, the senior stewardess asked "Did you hear that, Mr Long?" "Certainly did" I replied, not knowing what I was letting myself in for.

"There, I had better advise the Captain" picking up the intercom telephone, she said "Captain, there is an aircraft wishing to overtake us, (pause) very good Sir" Addressing the junior on only her second flight after Training School, the senior said

"Right young lady, you will have gone through this in Training School, so it will come as no surprise. Mr Long, you are nice and heavy, would you be kind enough to help?" Agreeing, I got out of my seat and stepped into the Galley where the senior was unpacking the Emergency Kit. she took a harness which had a very long rope attached to it. She made the junior put on the harness, passed the rope around her own waist while asking me to act as anchor, tying the end to my belt. She then told the junior, to place her toes on the leading edge of the aluminium bar set in the floor where the door joins it. "Now on my command, you open the door, lean out and wave the aircraft to overtake us. Got It?" The terrified junior was speechless, croaking out her protestations and claims of never having been taught this procedure. We two had a hell of a job suppressing our laughter. Even when assured that it was only a joke.

The poor junior was unable to give any service.

 # THE GIANT COCKROACH

The BAC 1-11 had just pushed back at Glasgow, with a full load of business breakfast passenger for Gatwick. The bar stewardess' reported to the senior stewardess, a lovely unflappable Scots lass. "Something moved in the hat rack when I looked in just now". The senior was very doubtful, but decided to check for herself. As she looked over the hat rack rim, she saw an enormous cockroach.

Controlling her reaction, she walked quickly to the Flight Deck. As she informed the captain of what she had seen, the First Officer came in with "There, skipper, I was right *and* not pissed, something did move across our dash board"

With the aircraft at Run Up and he had 119 business passengers on board, the captain decided to, say nothing and proceed to Gatwick. It was unlikely anyone would see the thing.

The 1-11, had been on a 6 month 'DRY' Lease to an African airline, who reported that they had fumigated it the day before it was to return to London.

At Gatwick, B.C.A.L's Engineering did their own fumigation. The afternoon it was being signed out to Line Duties, an engineer spotted a cockroach. The aircraft was immediately given a double dose fumigation, thoroughly checked and signed out. In spite of this high powered treatment the cockroach had survived. In fact, they are the most durable and resistant of creatures. They are the only creatures known to have survived the Hiroshima Atomic Bomb explosion.

A BUSINESS CLASS SEAT

A (very frequent) British Caledonian flyer wrote to the company complimenting them on the comfort of their new Business Class seats. He said that he had considerable difficulty in sleeping in any bed but none whatsoever in those seats. "I sleep like a log" he wrote.

The company saw an ideal opportunity to show their appreciation of his patronage, loyalty and kindness in writing by presenting him with such a seat and having it installed in his bedroom. They believed, that the national media would pick up the story which would go some considerable way to paying for the exercise. In the event, not only the national but a wide breath of the international media 'used' it.

The passenger was absolutely delighted, as were Field-Sales World Wide who used it extensively in their Public Relations and Sales pitch.

 ## THE CHEONG SAM

Another B.C.A.L regular to Hong Kong was married to a lass who very much wanted a Cheong Sam (Chinese style slim, dress with high neck and long slits up the legs).

Each time he left for Hong Kong, she asked him to bring one back., each time he returned, he had to apologies for having forgotten. He was, he claimed, so busy.

45

At Kai Tak about to join the DC10/30 for Gatwick, an announcement advised that the aircraft had a snag and that there would be a delay of about two hours. Our man decided to take a walk around the 'air side' concourse shops. In one, he spotted a dumb mannequin modelling the very dress.

Delighted, he asked for his wife's size which he kept note of in his Filofax, sadly the shop was out of stock but the enterprising owner asked, 'Does your wife dress make. If she has only the slightest knowledge, I have the simplest of patterns. I also will give you a very special price on some beautiful black silk?

On arrival back home, our man confessed that he had again forgotten until at the airport where he bought all the goodies for her.

His wife almost immediately set to making a beautiful dress. She embroidered a magnificent motif in Chinese characters down from her left shoulder to her breast. Her husband was very proud, and said that he would take her to the best Chinese restaurant in London where his company did a great deal of entertaining.

On the evening of the celebration, as they walked into the restaurant, they removed their top coats, the young waiters started to giggle. "What is wrong? the husband asked but no one responded as the giggling carried on. Again the pair asked, what was wrong, the wife felt, that in spite of her diligence, she had made some ghastly error.

Getting nowhere, they demanded to speak to the Maitre d'.

"We have repeatedly asked what is causing such hilarity amongst your junior waiters, but none will explain, unless you explain, we will leave and I will ensure that my company no longer patronise your establishment."

The Maitre d' apologised profusely for the rude behaviour of his peasant staff. However, he could understand what amused them.
Madam's dress is perfect, but from where did she get the beautifully embroidered motif?
"Out of a book", the wife replied.
"A cookery book? the Maitre d' queried.
"Yes" she replied with a quizzical look in her eyes.
"Ah so! madam, you motif says: Try me with cream, I am delicious!"

TOMATO KETCHUP

When my wife was a B.O.A.C stewardess (c 1950), early in her career, she was operating a service from New York to London. Whilst preparations were in hand for dinner, a child of about six, kept coming up to the galley becoming a damned nuisance. He was repeatedly taken back to his mother, with requests for him to be kept under control. There simply was none. All the cabin staff heard was "Wait until your father hears about this".

After 10 minutes, the 'monster' was back in the galley.

The chief steward, personally took the child back to his mother and very firmly told her, "that something drastic might happen to her child, if he is not kept under control". Sure enough, inside 10 minutes, he was back yet again. The 'chief' grabbed the child by the collar, at the same time his elbow hit a tray of silverware making an almighty clatter. it was heard throughout the cabin.

He then took a bottle of Tomato Ketchup and emptied it all over the child.

Grabbing a fist full of napkins, he marched the child through the cabin back to his mother.
"Now look what he has done madam, kindly keep your offspring under control before something more dramatic happens to him"

The child was not allowed to stir another muscle!

"DON'T TELL MY ..."

A steward I knew with a Middle Eastern carrier, told me, that if you saw two Arabs from The Gulf in Economy class, they will, relatively speaking, not be too well off and they would be devout Muslims.

On a flight to London , he went out into the cabin to ask who would like a beverage. Two Arab passengers, a father and his adult son sitting together ordered 7UP' with ice. As my friend continued his round, the father went to the toilet. The son beckoned to the steward "When you bring our drinks, please put a gin in mine but say nothing to my father" he whispered.
"No problem sir, your drink will have a slice of lemon in it" the steward assured him. He carried on taking orders.

When the steward returned to the galley and was making up his tray, the father came out of the nearby toilet. He sidled up to him looking carefully at his son, he said "Excuse me young man, but when you bring our drinks, please put a vodka into mine but say nothing to my son. This is very important". The steward said he clearly understood and that his drink would be plain, your son will have a slice of lemon to differentiate. For the remainder of the flight, all either passenger would say was "same again please".

When they arrived at Gatwick, they were both well 'oiled'. Oiled, Arabs, get it? However, each was convinced that his companion was drunk!

THE FLAMING PRESS

Back in 1956, the old Colonel was last to board the B.O.A.C Argonaut for Nairobi at Heathrow.

He was surprised and annoyed to see that the aircraft was not merely full, there were only eight adult passengers on board. The flight was routing Rome, Cairo, Khartoum, Entebbe, Nairobi. and the Colonel asked the Chief Steward where all the youngsters were destined.

In his heart, he hoped they would disembark at Rome, his head told him that he had miscalculated the end of term and that they were all going to East Africa. The Chief confirmed this, with 85% Kenya, the rest Uganda. He was unconcerned because he and his crew were to 'layover' in Rome.

The Colonel, resigning himself to the horrors of such a flight, requested *The Times* (then the Air Mail edition was printed on extremely light and flimsy paper) and a continuous supply of G & T's without ice. He resolved to read every word of the newspaper, from top left corner page one, to bottom right last page.

Being a Friday, it was a 'heavy' edition. Departure time was 1330 and Rome was over four hours away. An hour out from Rome, the children became restless, it was too early to sleep, they looked for something else to occupy themselves.

The Colonel had two pages to finish and he was well oiled. Suddenly, The Times went up in flames. One little 'darling' had crawled up the aisle and set a lighted match to the bottom of the highly inflammable newspaper.

"WHEN PHOEBE SETS FIRE TO THE XMAS TREE, YOU SQUIRT IT WITH THE 100 OCTANE,"

Roy CALDERON

A DEATH ON BOARD

It used to be a requirement, that if a death occurred on board an aircraft before it reached the halfway point of its flight (The Point of No Return), the aircraft had to return to its point of origin.

When my wife was a novice stewardess with B.O.A.C she learnt this in her training. On one of her first flights to New York, they were carrying a consignment of 'day old chicks', stored between the Radio Officer's panel and the Galley. The mortality rate, in the 50's was very high. Thankfully today it is much improved. However, some airlines will not carry them unless, the shipper signs an indemnity releasing the airline from all responsibility

Back to Anne- a few of the chicks legs were rather wobbly and the Chief Steward instructed Anne personally to take charge of their welfare. The chicks slowly deteriorated and because the 'Chief was very concerned', he suggested they be placed in the oven which MUST be kept on a very low heat. 'With that wretched law, they have to be kept alive until they past the P o N Return.

Further, it was in Anne's interest to keep them alive until arrival in N.Y because a death on board called for the completion of reams of forms, the N.Y authorities were particularly demanding. As you will have gathered, their flight was almost empty and some chicks died. Not until they landed, did the 'Chief' put her out of her misery.

 # PARROTS

General Manager West Africa Region (GMWAR) was visiting London flying on board one of his aircraft. Seated next to him in First Class, was a passenger who kept fiddling with his hand baggage. Eventually, the passenger asked GMWAR if he was going to eat that last piece of celery on his plate. GMWAR suggested that if he wanted more, all he had to do, was ask. "I would prefer to use that which will be thrown away, rather than request a fresh piece. You see, I want it for the parrots in my hand baggage. Each time I go on leave, twice a year, I take two young parrots. Paying no freight, import charges and Customs duties, I sell them to a pet shop and make more than enough to pay for my holiday". GMWAR just nodded and passed his celery.

After the meal had been cleared away, GMWAR took out a file and a calculator and started to work on a report. He explained to his travelling companion, 'It must be ready before we land'. An hour later, the passenger with the parrots, excused himself to visit the toilet.

On his return, he found a business card had been left on the seat divide. It was annotated 'P.T.O'. The reverse read: '12 years x 2 = 24 visits carrying 48 parrots. Average charge for a parrot in an R.S.P.C.A cage weighing 3 Kilos Lagos

– London £6 per kilo x 3 = 18 x 48 = £864. Kindly forward your cheque to our Cargo Revenue Account who will be anticipating it. Nothing will be said to H.M Customs providing that you guarantee no further such imports.

THE ROTARIAN

Rotary Clubs strive to have a Guest Speaker at three of their four monthly meetings. The fourth is devoted to club business. When difficulty in finding a speaker is encountered, not an uncommon occurrence, a member is asked to speak. Some times they speak on their job, in fact they may choose any subject.

On one occasion of difficulty, a member, well known for his amorous claims, particularly in his earlier years, was invited to speak 'on sex'.

He collected some books from the library and bought a few 'girlie' magazines to research his subject. However, he was shy of his wife finding out and to hide his study books, he bought a very large reference book on flying, which would mask his books. In his study, with his flying book facing the door, he read avidly. His wife, looking in asked, "What are you doing?". "I have to give a talk at Rotary on flying. I must study hard, it is on Thursday".

Two days after the lunch, the Club President, walking along the High Street, bumped into the 'speaker's' wife, he greeted her with. "Oh Margaret, we had a super talk from John on Thursday. he really appears to be an expert in his subject". Margaret with a smile of query, was impressed. "I'm glad to hear that, considering he has only been up twice. The first time he was sick, the second he time he fainted!"

"IF YOU WOULD ...."

The all to frequent argument at 'Check In' relates to Excess Baggage. The lies told by passengers, trying to avoid paying for their excess are legion. Sadly the attitude of many such passengers, frequently becomes aggressive, often nasty.

One American passenger had an enormous piece of baggage which not only put him well overweight, it was better suited for the hold rather than the cabin. He insisted that he carry the bag and that it was not subject to excess charge.

The 'Check In Agent' would not agree and the passenger insisted on seeing the Duty Officer. After 10 minutes of unreasonable argument by the passenger, he shouted "You know exactly what you can do with your excess charges, I will not leave it behind".

The Duty Officer, literally at the end of his tether, replied "If you would care to do the same with you hand baggage sir, you may take it with you".

PRESSURISE

On two flight deck crew aircraft, at airports where no ground engineer was on duty, one pilot will do 'the walk around', the engineering check.

Often they do not have a plug in microphone/headset to facilitate communication from under the aircraft to the flight deck. Further, the outside noises were frequently too loud to permit direct voice communication.

Sign language often becomes the only alternative to endlessly climbing up and down the aircraft steps to and from the cockpit, every time they needed to talk. This also applies to other airport staff. Two nice illustrations are:

"I DUNNO..... MAYBE ITS SOMETHING TO DO WITH THE PRESSURIZATION ....?"

The first

When doing the walk around around, the pilot under the aircraft, would bang on the hold to attract attention. When he had the attention of his colleague, he then placed his thumbs close to his ears and raised his index and second fingers on and off his eyes lids. Most catch on quickly.

A captain, under his Airbus at an Arabain Gulf station, was getting nowhere with his First Officer. After he had to climbed the steps for the third time to clarify signs, he said "You will have to learn English with an English accent, your bloody Spanish accent just will not do"

"Signor Capitano, I do nota understand whata you try to tella me"
"Watch carefully, what am I doing Pancho?"
"You putta your fingers ona you eyes, yes?" replied Pancho.
"No, No its PRESS your EYES, get it? P R E S S U R I S E the hydraulics for me to test." OK?

The second.

When the fuelling bowser is returning to its depot, the driver might observe an unscheduled aircraft on the ramp. After attracting attention from a distance, the driver will tightly close the second, third and fourth fingers of his hand which he then raises above his head and lowers his thumb in and out of his mouth. This asks the crew if they need fuel, e.g. "Need a drink?"

JUST PASSING THROUGH?

A passenger who was transiting between London's airports could not seem accept that it was not like his beloved Boston's one international airport. At both Heathrow and Gatwick, the worlds' two busiest international airports, one could do the same *providing* the transfer was *within that airport*. If one had to transfer between them, it was no different to transferring between any two, e.g. Kennedy and La Guardia or Newark. If an international arrival was involved, Customs and Immigration had to be cleared at the first point of entry.

His baggage had been temporarily mishandled from Boston causing him to have barely enough time to make his connection at Gatwick for Lagos. Having slept through breakfast on the transatlantic flight, he planned to eat at Gatwick. Now there was insufficient time. As if this was not enough misfortune, At the Departure Gate, the shoulder strap on his cabin bag snapped crashing to the ground smashing his Duty Free Whiskey and spreading his possessions all over the floor.

To cap it all, he was asked to accept a change to his allocated seat to get a family together.

Exasperated, he shouted, "London's Airports are the arsehole of the world".

The Gate Agent to whom the remark was addressed replied "Just passing through are you sir?"

 ## SISTERS

In Sydney Australia, some Catholic Sister, ran a hospice in a sleazy quarter. Regrettably, their principal benefactor died suddenly without leaving a will. In spite of strenuous efforts to raise funds, they got nowhere near sufficient to their needs. A young novice told her assembled community, that she had a solution. Although fairly unusual, she asked to be heard. "We should have a red light fitted outside our front door, its presence would speak for itself. The older nuns were dismayed but since they were unable to come up with a viable alternative, they reluctantly agreed.

The first evening the light was illuminated, the young novice was assigned to the front door She had not long to wait for her first caller, a First Officer pilot.
"How much?, he demanded gruffly.
"Two hundred dollars" the novice advised.
"$200 exclaimed the man, that's a hell of a lot".
"Ah yes, but you see, this is something really special!"
she demurely told him.

Intrigued, the man paid up and was admitted. "Go straight through the cloister, climb the stairs, turn right at the top and enter the first door on the left"

The pilot did precisely as instructed. On entering the room, he was surprised to hear the door slam shut and lock. As he turned, he noticed that there was no handle on his side of the door, further there was a note in the middle of the door.

It read: "Please be advised, that you have been screwed by the Sisters".
The exit is directly behind you!

54

MISREADING THE SIGNS

One of British Caledonian's lovely Cale Girls told me of a beautiful misreading of the sign at Mutalla Mohamed airport Lagos.

Having come out of an aircraft jetty into the terminal, she saw a sign reading

"TO D FINGER".

Not until she saw the next sign, did she realise that it was not an error. The second sign read:

"TO C, D & E—FINGERS"!

MYSTERY OPERATION

The BR353, departed Gatwick some 2 hours 30 minutes late. It was scheduled to operate Gatwick–Banjul–Freetown–Robertsfield and vice versa.

In an endeavour to make up time, we decided to omit the second call at Freetown. This meant that all passengers ex–Freetown to Banjul and London, would have to depart Lungi Airport at 2100, *instead* of the scheduled time of 2240. After briefing our passengers they were totally confused. e.g. They were required to leave their homes 2 hours earlier than planned, to catch a plane that was running 2 hours 30 minutes late but would nonetheless take off from Freetown some 1hr 40 mins earlier than the scheduled time. It would still arrive Gatwick 40 mins late, providing that it kept to the new schedule!

To illustrate N.B All times G.M.T

Scheduled Operation		**STATIONS**	**Rescheduled** Operation..
2240	(dep)	FREETOWN	2100 (dep) – **100mins:**
		ROBERTSFIELD	2200 (arr)
		ROBERTSFIELD	2300 (dep)
2350	(arr)	BANJUL	0130 (arr)
0050	(dep)	BANJUL	0230 (dep)
0630	(arr)	GATWICK	0710 (arr) + **40mins:**

TWO CHRISTMASES

One Christmas season in the 80's, K.L.M. Freetown enjoyed two Christmas days within a fortnight. The first was normal on Dec 25th, the second on Jan 8th.

When their flight of the 7th Jan arrived from Amsterdam, they had to complete 35 Property Irregularity Reports covering 68 pieces of missing bags. When completed, the meagre staff were exhausted.

Next day at 1000hrs, the staff were preparing for their northbound operation. They moved their baggage containers into position in readiness for loading. As they lifted the heavy blue plastic 'doors', there to their relief, they discovered all the missing bags. The Loaders had simply not Off Loaded.

A new rule was said to have been made by the hundreds of people who illegally took short cuts through the airport. Security was so bad, that these workers simply walked right through the Ramp, Fuelling and V.I.P areas.

The 'RULE' was 'never' walk past a baggage container, without lifting the 'door' to see if anyone had left them a bag or two.

GETTING YOUR HANDS DIRTY

One of my first neighbours in Nairobi in 1956, was a super Northern Irishman by the name of Sam Dickson. He had a lovely wife called Margaret and two young daughters Patricia and Barbara. Sam, a Licensed Avionics and Radio Engineer (with East African), taught me what little I know about motor car engineering. Sam was often taken to task by non engineering staff for always helping me but no one else. Mostly Sam ignored these cracks.

I was told that one day, he was confronted by a senior colleague, rather annoyed who asked 'Why do you help Long, but no one else?"

"It is very simple, Denis will put on overalls and get his hands dirty, no one else is prepared to do that" said Sam in his broad Irish brogue.

One afternoon at Wilson Airfield, where E.A.A maintained its DC3 and smaller aircraft, Sam was working on a DC3. He was lying on his back, in the nose cone of the aircraft, with his head and shoulders out in space. Sam needed a tool. as he turned to reach for it, he glanced towards the Hangar

Doors which were slightly open. Across the gap, was the tummy of a large dog. Sam, a great dog lover, was anxious to take a closer look. He climbed down and out of the DC3 and walked over to the doors. Half way across, 'the dog' moved, Sam realised, that he had never seen a dog, with a tuft of hair at the end of its tail. His 'dog', was in fact, a lion. Sam beat a hasty retreat to the safety of his aircraft .N.B. Wilson airport, Africa's busiest General Aviation airport, literally boarders the Royal Nairobi National Game Park.

THE DRIVE-IN

About the same time as Sam Dickson saw his 'dog' at the hangar, my wife Anne and I visited Nairobi's Belle View Drive In. Usually, I would ask Anne what she wanted from the cafeteria. I would saunter over and place our order.

This particular evening I acted 'stroppy', telling her that it was about time she took her turn on the chore. Annoyed, Anne went over to the counter. On her return, I asked "See any lions?" producing a copy of the East African Standard of that day, its headlines read:

'LION WALKS THROUGH BELLE VIEW'

The Drive In, was also situated on the Game Park boundary but at the East Side. The previous nights' visit of the lion, (a very unusual event), finished with the carcass of a goat being dragged by a Land Rover on a long lead. It enticed the lion back into the Game Park where he belonged and remained.

CHOLERA

The medical men and women were beaten, there was no doubt their patient had the dreaded Cholera but where from? He had never set foot outside of his very remote village, what's more, no one from the village had travelled more that 50 Kilometres in the past five years.

They had no visitors from anywhere past 35 kilometres over the same period. The problem could not have fallen from heaven, said a technician but the Professor in charge had different thoughts. He called the Department of Civil Aviation in Budapest and after explaining his dilemma, requested details of all aircraft which overflew the village. He wanted to know, a) Time. b) Type of aircraft. c) Nationality. d) Complete routing.

After receiving the report, he established that a 747 flew over the village at about 0430 local time four days a week. it was en route from Asia to a Western European Capital. The professor deduced that passengers visited the toilet and after washing their hands, the hand basin water was (as is usual) let out of the aircraft into the air below. Further investigation confirmed this theory.

JET STREAM

In 1969 at an Asian airport, a great tragedy was narrowly averted because of a major hold up on the runway!

A 1649A *Super Constellation* of a major airline, known to many as a 'JETSTREAM' was incorrectly fuelled with **JET A1 fuel.**

The 'JETSTREAM' had compound engines requiring AVGAS (AVIATION GASOLINE) like highly supped up car fuel.

JET A1, is for pure jet engines, basically a paraffin.

Because of runway congestion, the 'Connie' had to sit in the 'HOLD' position awaiting clearance. Mercifully, the hold up was long enough for the Jet fuel to reach the engines, one of which stalled.

Had the aircraft taken off, when the wrong fuel reached the engines in flight - there would have been no more flight. The engines would close down and the aircraft would have fallen out of the sky.

 # 'THAT'S THE SEVEN OF YOU'

In 1953, I was doing a 7 day relief in Rome. For what reason I cannot recall, I was required by my Duty Officer personally to deliver a message to the Captain of the next B.O.A.C aircraft out. The Captain, with his crew, were in the Quirinale Hotel, located at the head of the via Nazionale.

Arriving at the hotel, I was directed by reception to the breakfast room where, I spotted the crew sitting together in a corner. As I approached them, it was clear that the Captain was rather annoyed. Suddenly, the First Officer brushed past me in somewhat of a hurry. As he reached the table, he sheepishly apologised to the Captain for being late. The Captain grunted his disapproval.

In the mid 50's, captains considered themselves 'gods'. One rarely spoke to them until they spoke to you. I stood waiting my turn.

Just as I was about deliver my message, 'the stewardess' waltzed in (in those days, there was only one per crew). The Captain threw a glance at her, that would have killed a lesser being. Instead of demurely apologising for her late arrival, she haughtily said "Ah well, that's the seven of you".

I stood there with my mouth wide open until, I heard the captain bellow at me, "Well young man, what exactly do you want?" For the life of me, for a few seconds I could not remember.

N.B In the 1950's , a London Hong Kong crew, round trip was about 11 days.

"NOW THAT THE ....."

In 1961, Central African Airways introduced a novel Public Address message to departing passengers at the end of their flights.It ran:

LADIES and GENTLEMEN,
WELCOME TO ....,
NOW THAT THE SAFEST PART OF YOUR
JOURNEY IS OVER—
PLEASE *DRIVE HOME VERY* CAREFULLY.

 ## IF YOU "HAD FOUR ..."

Two vultures were circling at about 12,000ft just north of Entebbe, when a British United Airways VC10 passed overhead, bound for London.

The two birds, lost their stability and dropped several thousand feet. Charlie dropped much further than Fred.

When Charlie regained the same altitude as Fred, he asked "What the hell was that, Fred?"

"I dunno, said Fred, what I do know is, that if you had four *backsides all on fire,* you my friend would definitely be going that fast!"

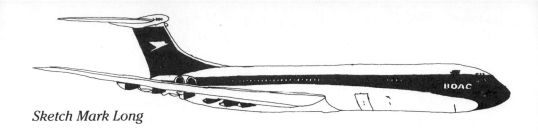

Sketch Mark Long

THE 'SICK' VC10

The BR211 landed at Entebbe from Gatwick en route to Lusaka. An 'oleo' leg problem had caused the nose wheel unit to lock, making it impossible for the aircraft to taxi onto the Ramp and park. Engineers, using a jack on wheels and a Towmaster managed to get the VC10 off the runway and onto the Ramp which reopened the airport.

They estimated a 15 hour delay.

With 8 hours, including the turn around at Lusaka ahead of us before the aircraft, was due back to operate Entebbe–London, I decided to try to organise a charter to operate the Entebbe –Lusaka–Entebbe sectors.

To this end, I called East African Airways to enquire of the availability of a DC9 aircraft. This would take the London–Lusaka, Entebbe–Lusaka, Lusaka –Entebbe and Lusaka–London loads over the problematic sectors and all northbound passengers could then join the VC10 Entebbe–London.

Try as I may, I could not get through to East African Charter Department and called my opposite number 'Denny' Dennison in Nairobi, requesting him to liaise with E.A.A. Denny advised that E.A.A had no aircraft available for charter capable of the loads I had a requirement for.

Just as I was about to put down the phone, 5X-UVA, a Super VC10 of E.A.A landed. With Entebbe airport absolutely deserted, save for my stranded passengers. I asked the E.A.A Service Controller "Where is your 10 going? "Damned if I know, it is not on my Mayfly" he replied.

Quickly, I asked Denny to recall E.A.A Ops: and ask them what the hell 'Uniform Victor Alpha' is doing in Entebbe. Reluctant to call E.A.A, Denny asked "What on earth do you think it is doing there?" "That is precisely the point There

60

is no one here and it is not on the Mayfly. Furthermore there are no passengers at 'Check In'. Please just do as I ask" I pleaded. "E.A.A say, its to operate a Jeddah charter" Denny advised. Anyone who has had the misfortune to be at an airport when a large aircraft is about to leave on such an operation will know, that for every passenger travelling four or five relatives and or friends are there to see them off. Reiterating the total lack of anyone at Check In, I again asked Denny to ascertain who is the charterer. I prayed that it would be a Uganda agent with whom I could talk directly. It was down to a Kampala Travel Agent. On checking I learned that he had cancelled his contract some six weeks earlier!

I requested Denny to "Offer E.A.A an Entebbe–Lusaka–Entebbe charter on two very strict conditions.

a) I would take it at the DC9 hourly rate. I had no need for the balance of seats.

b) I would not pay positioning fees Nairobi–Entebbe–Nairobi. East African were in a hole and accepted.

The only condition I had to accept was that the aircraft was catered for a Jeddah charter, predominantly Asian food. In those days, not so widely accepted in the U.K as it is today. However East Africa residents would be no problem.

Whatever, we had no choice, it was Asian food or no charter.

The cabin staff were asked to explain the problem to their passengers over the P/A but pleaded with me to do so. There were some 12 passengers in First Class, I decided to brief them face to face. The Economy Class passengers I briefed over the P/A.

Having explained to the First Class passengers how an Agent had cancelled but that E.A.A had not taken the flight off the schedule. They had positioned it to Entebbe fully catered for Jeddah. Some American passengers started to try to give me a hard time. Amongst the Brits, was Edward du Cann, a prominent M.P and then Leader of the very influential 1922 Committee of the House of Commons.

He stood up and said "While I clearly have no authority to speak on behalf of anyone other than those in my own party, I wish it to be known, that ALL in my group are exceedingly grateful and impressed by Mr Long's efforts. Few show such care, dedication and attention to the well being of their charges". Not another word was heard from the Americans.

BRADLEY'S LOG

Circa 1956, the Duty Terminal Controller, in British European Airways, was a former Royal Air Force Officer, of Polish origin, who changed his name to Bradley. As was normal, a log of all aircraft movements, with reasons for any delays written alongside the affected flight was kept.

I took over as Night Duty Controller, at an extremely busy time, and the handover was very quick.

During the night, it was the responsibility of the night controller to, update the 'MAYFLY' (The list of flights which MAY-FLY in the 24 hours between the coming 0500 & 0459, Hence MAY-FLY said it all).

To up date the MAYFLY, one referred to the log for details of any changes to be added to the next days' scheduled. One entry had not only me, but all my colleagues on duty totally confused. It read:
BE152 NIGHT STOPPING ROME DUE CREW **FOR TEA.**
It should have read: DUE CREW **FATIGUE!**

The crew had suffered a 4 hour delay at Rome and had run out of their allotted Duty Hours for that day from London to Athens.

WHAT A CAPTAIN!

Personally, I never met the legendary and well loved man, the centre of numerous pranks, much talked of and enjoyed in B.E.A circa 1948-50. I will report on seven of his alleged lovely pranks.

1. His favourite targets were grumpy businessmen who flew the German Domestic sectors of B.E.A. They were forever complaining, sometimes justifiably but mostly not. On one occasion, he came out of his cockpit, put his fingers into his mouth and whistled in a fashion more associated with sports grounds. "I" he said to his startled passengers, "I hear that you lot have complained at the lack of entertainment by our Captains". With that, he took a red and white sock cap out of his pocket and donned it. He rolled up his trouser legs to display matching socks. From his pocket, he produced an harmonica on which he played a jig, to which he danced. At the finish, he asked "Are you now happy and satisfied with the entertainment?"

2. One day he walked through the cabin, in full uniform of course, wearing dark glasses and tapping each row with a white stick. You can imagine the reaction of the passengers.

3. It was his occasional pass time, to walk through the cabin carrying a scrap-book type book with in very large letters 'HOW TO FLY in 6 EASY LESSONS'. He would sit in the last row of the cabin and studiously read the book.

4. During those summer months, B.E.A Flight Deck crew wore gaberdine jackets and trousers, being 'light weight'. At Glasgow early one morning, he was briefed that Northolt (then London's second airport) had heavy fog. It was expected to 'burn off' 45 minutes after his scheduled time of arrival. He went out to his DC3 ahead of his passenger. There he put on his tweed jacket and took off his company tie. He sat reading his newspaper awaiting the boarding of his passengers. He had instructed Passenger Services to 'Bring them out in 20 minutes, but say nothing about any delay. With no announcement, having been made, in a raised and very clear voice he said "What the hell are this lot up to this morning?" No one responded.

He repeated this remark a few minutes later adding, "If they do not get it together I guess I will have to fly the bloody thing!" The passengers on either side of him, smiled nervously.

Eventually, he said "That's it, we are off" making his way forward to the cockpit after demanding that the Stewardess close the door. In typical British fashion, in spite of being very concerned - not a soul made any attempt to dissuade him. The 'Dakota's engines spluttered to life, it taxied out and took off. Shortly after they were airborne, he appeared in full uniform of course.

5. He was renowned for his teasing young ladies, obviously impressed by the glamour of his uniform. He would lean over the back of a seat, in front of them, displaying his eight thick gold rings on his two sleeves. After chatting to the girls for some time. he, in the knowledge that they were bound for Rome would take his leave of them with "You must excuse me ladies, we must commence our 'let down' into Copenhagen in 4 minutes, I will be needed on the Flight Deck", with that he was gone. Panic immediately set in with the girls. Copenhagen, *Copenhagen,* **Copenhagen!!** what is he saying Copenhagen, we are going to Rome". They would press the call button while desperately trying to think what they were going to do. The steward, knowing what his captain got up to, took his time. The call button was rung repeatedly. When he arrived, the girls told him their plight. he would nonchalantly reply, "Pay no attention to him, he is never certain of where we are going!" Most reassuring.

6. Another day he was waiting in the 'hold' position for take off clearance. An Aer Lingus captain in the 'zone' coming into Northolt, was practising the then new phonetic alphabet. "Northolt, Northolt this is Aer Lingus Foxtrot Tango this, and Foxtrot Tango that", it never seemed to end. our friend switched on his radio with Control this is Uncle George, kindly advise Victor Sylvester (then a very popular strict tempo dance band leader) that when he is finished his B for Bloody, D for Dancing lesson I for Item am waiting to 'T' for take 'O' for off.'

7. On another occasion, he was checking out a junior pilot. Having landed during a very busy period, he was asked to wait in the far corner of the 'Hold Area'. Just over the fence, were a bunch of youngsters playing football. The story goes, that he reduced his engines to 'idle', opened his cockpit window and shouted at the boys "Scuse me, but am I all right for Northolt?" The boys politely advised "Yeah guv, you've made it".

 **ALL FOREIGNERS**

An Airport Manager based in Southern Africa had a rather unique problem.

It was of his own making, none of his five children, his wife, nor himself were born in the same country. Each held a passport of their country of their birth.

All were different! He *thought this amusing* until, instead of going home for his vacations, they wanted to see pastures new. It caused tremendous difficulties with at least one visa requirement no matter where they wanted to go. In discussion, a friend suggested that he, as the 'father' having an Irish Grandmother, he and all the children should be able to secure Irish Passports. Possibly the Irish might, under the circumstance, grant Irish Citizenship to his wife. He approached the Irish Embassy in Pretoria who in turn asked Dublin. In time Dublin replied granting permission to issue all seven with Irish Passports. From then on, all or none required a visa.

FOOTNOTE. Is it any wonder St. Jack Charlton when Ireland Soccer Team Manager did so well?

 **'LONG ODDS'**

A gentleman, who was due to visit his daughter in Australia, had only sufficient time available to fly. Sadly he was terrified that someone would put a bomb on his aircraft.

He consulted a mathematician, asking him to work out the odds. After a few days, he went back to learn what they were.

He was counselled, "Statistics prove, that they are about 5.5 million to one'. The mathematician was surprised to observe a look of some concern on his client's face.

"I am not happy, the odds are not long enough, I do not think I will go" said the passenger.

Concerned, the consultant suggested that if he took a bomb with him, the odds would lengthen to 24.6 million to one against another bomb being on board!

The passenger travelled, by air, to see his daughter.

VIKINGS & VIKINGS

In 1951 I was on loan to Heathrow, assigned to Ramp duties, a job I had previously done. Today they are known as Red Caps.

With staff shortages, we were pushed, it was no time for joking around. We were working the Bath Road side of the airport and Captain Jim Hartley's Viking service was on Stand '1' at the far end of the Ramp. He was operating the BE323 to Paris, scheduled departure 0800.

Just as I cleared the Brussels, Jim called me on my radio advising that the had a 'MAG DROP', a problem with a magneto. I was requested to 'hold his passengers'. I informed the Departure Gate accordingly. For the minute, it gave me a little breathing space. However, I was aware, that once serviceable, I would have to squeeze in the *extra* departure.

After about 15 minutes, Jim called up saying "Put them on Denis'. I, in turn instructed Departures. Being very busy, I paid little attention to coach movements across the Ramp. After about 10 minutes, Jim came on repeating his request. I apologised for the delay, promising to get on to it at once.

Departures Supervisor, was quite haughty when I informed her that I was not out on the Ramp entertaining the birds. "Where the hell are his passengers?" I demanded.

"They left within a minute of your request, hold on I'll check", the supervisor grunted. "On board", was all she came back with.

I immediately thought that Jim had a further problem, and that whilst waiting engineering clearance, he would while away his time bating me.

"I know you have them Jim, please no joking about, we are desperately busy" "Mr LONG, I am ready to go for all of 15 minutes, whilst I am sympathetic to your problems, I am not sitting around here until you think fit to dispatch me" "Yes Captain Hartley, my apologies Captain Hartley I will personally sort it right now". I called the Gate and asked for the supervisor to have the girl who advised her that the passengers were boarded to await my arrival. At the Gate, I asked her precisely where she had taken the BE323 passengers. "To the VIKING. I personally helped them settle in on board" she sarcastically replied.

"Right lass, get on to the back of my Lambretta, you can speak to the Captain face to face" I told her.

As I roared down the Ramp (our scooters were souped up to use Avgas which really made them shift) passing many parked aircraft, my passenger shouted,

"They are on the Viking" waving her arm towards an aircraft we were passing.

"That my girl, is NOT a Viking, its a DC4" What the hell I thought, if they are on that, they are on the wrong aircraft. I called Jim explaining and promising to switch them over ASAP. Transport was instructed to provide a coach immediately.

I then explained to the girl "A Viking aircraft sits on its tail, whereas a DC4 sits on its nose wheel".

By this time the coach arrived and we transferred the passengers very quickly. I asked the driver "Who the hell drove the passengers out to the DC4?" He replied "I did, Denis". "But you knew full well that they were bound for Paris on B.E.A, that they were to fly on a Viking and that we have no DC4s". "S'right", he grinned.

"Then why on earth did you let her carry on?" I was exasperated."That one, is the snootiest of the lot. She treats us drivers like dirt. She ordered me to stop at the DC4, even help her push the steps up to the aircraft, open the door and shepherd the passengers on board. I simply did as ordered "But its not your job" I interjected "S'right but now she has to face the music", he grinned.

The problem was caused for two reasons, the girl's stupid attitude towards our terrific drivers and because Scandinavian Airlines call all their aircraft VIKINGS, including today's Airbuses and B747's all their aircraft are named after their historic Vikings heroes. One of their 747's is conveniently named 'HUGE VIKING'. However, I understand that Huge is a Forename in Scandinavia.

Sketch Mark Long

A Viking sitting on its tail

UGANDA's 1ST 'JUMBO' JET CHARTER

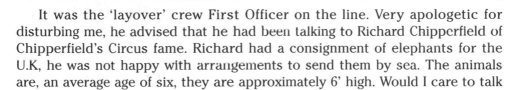

It was the 'layover' crew First Officer on the line. Very apologetic for disturbing me, he advised that he had been talking to Richard Chipperfield of Chipperfield's Circus fame. Richard had a consignment of elephants for the U.K, he was not happy with arrangements to send them by sea. The animals are, an average age of six, they are approximately 6' high. Would I care to talk to him? "

I thanked the First Officer and in spite of it being 1830 Saturday, with a dinner party organised, I drove the 19 miles straight out to Entebbe.

I discovered that Chipperfield had 24 such elephants together with a selection of other animals and large birds which were for Zoos.

Head Office came up with a competitive quote and we were in business. When our B707 had departed for U.K, I issued a news release:

'WITH 24 ELEPHANTS, 2 ZEBRAS, A CHEETAH, and 6 CROWN CRANES. B.C.A.L OPERATES THE VERY FIRST 'JUMBO' JET CHARTER FROM ENTEBBE'

It was exceptionally well received by both the press and the public. Two days before the operation was due to take place, some lunatic at Head Office Gatwick London (knowing precisely what the consignment was) advised me by telex, that they planned a publicity stunt. They were going to 'walk the elephants, tail to trunk from the aircraft to the freight shed'. Of course Telecommunications to the U.K promptly went down and stayed down for some time. I had to call our friends at the British Diplomatic Mission to radio London and ask them to instruct Gatwick not to be so stupid. The Elephants were *wild,* we had to secure R.S.P.C.A permission to carry them in boxes designed to greatly inhibit their movements because of this. The fact that they were owned by Chipperfields, did not mean that they were circus trained.

"I don't know, better ask Mr Long in Entebbe"

THE BCAL ARK

Some months later, as a result of our success with Uganda's First 'Jumbo' Jet flight, I was approached to operate another animal freight charter. It being infinitely more comfortable for the animals than a sea journey from 35-56 days. I had to think of a new press release 'title', if I was to stand any chance of getting this accepted by the media.I decided on:

**"WITH 200 MONKEYS, 2 GIRAFFE (babies),
5 ZEBRA, 6 CROWN CRANES, 4 CHEETAHS,
6 IMPALA IN THE HOLDS, A SCOTTISH LION
ON THE TAIL and ESSO TIGERS in the TANKS,
THE B.C.A.L ARK LEFT for LONDON".**

Again, it was very well received by press and public.

 # TRUE COMPASSION

Captain Duncan Maclachlan, formerly of Singapore Malaysian Airlines, told me of the night he operated the last aircraft to get into Kai Tak Hong Kong through a typhoon which later closed the airport.

On entering the terminal building, he heard the tragic news of a B707 of B.O.A.C which had crashed on 'finals' into Tokyo harbour.

In the bar of their crew hotel, Machlachlan saw another B.O.A.C crew and commiserated with them on the loss of their colleagues.

Surprisingly, little response was forthcoming. Thinking that they had not heard him, he delicately repeated his words of compassion.

Eventually the B.O.A.C crew responded "Thanks, the really sad thing is, they were all junior to us!"

N.B For the uninitiated. Commercial Pilots normally, are promoted on the basis of qualifications and years of seniority.

BULLSHIT!

A variety of carriers in the 'zone' over New York's 'JFK' heard one of their number say "BULLSHIT" to an Air Traffic Controller's instruction. N.B. Strict adherence to procedural courteous discussion is always required.

The angry controller asked each aircraft under his control. In turn if he was 'guilty', intending to discipline the offender.

Their responses to his question ran -

American Airlines?	AA are negative on BULLSHIT.
British Airways?	BA are negative on BULLSHIT
United Airlines?	UA are negative on BULLSHIT
K.L.M?	KL are negative on BULLSHIT
Air Canada?	AC are negative on BULLSHIT

and so on until the controller thought that he recognised the offending voice say. "Guess you are negative on Bullshit!"

BULLSHIT THE EXPLANATION.

One of the 'A' class submarines in the British Navy launched in 1945 was **H.M.S AUROCHS.** An AUROCHS is an extinct Bison and the 'sub' was there after known to her crew as the *'WOOLLY BULLY'*.

Their crest was the head of this animal carrying the Latin motto:

'TAURUS EXCRETA SAPIENTUM FULCREAT'

which rather freely translates to :

"THE DUNG OF THE BULL CAUSES WISDOM TO FLEE"

but the crews translation recognised world-wide, was:

"BULLSHIT BAFFLES BRAINS"

'THE CAPTAIN HAS JUMPED'

In the 1950's, a South East Asian airline DC3 Captain and his First officer decided to play a practical joke on their stewardess while in flight.

They slid back the captain's window in the cockpit, let some 'freight lashing' out and re closed the window, allowing the lashing to bang on the side of the fuselage. The Captain then went and hid in the freight compartment situated immediately behind the cockpit, an unlit area.

The First Officer rang for the Stewardess. On arrival, he informed her of the 'tragedy' adding that the Captain's last words were that 'He had had enough of life and that he was jumping'. The F/O went on to say 'that he had little experience of this type of aircraft and apart from being unable to restrain the Captain, whilst flying the machine, he was worried about having to land it safely at destination.

Without uttering a word, the Stewardess left the cockpit with great haste. Seconds later, she returned with an absolutely huge Australian, whom she advised the F/O held a Private Pilot's Licence, he knew the DC3 quite well and would help.

On hearing this, and foreseeing problems, the Captain climbed out of the freight compartment. The startled Aussie let fly a super right cross, knocking the Captain unconscious.

THE YACHT MAST

It was an essential and much needed part if their racing dinghy was to be able to compete in the National Championships of Nigeria. The only way to get it to Lagos was to air freight it.

B.C.A.L was contacted and advised of the importance of the mast arriving a.s.a.p and in one piece. The booking was effected on the next B707 freighter to Lagos. Cargo Planning reckoned that if the 30' mast were raised on two gantries positioned
  a) Immediately parallel and very close to the cockpit.
  b) Some 15' to the rear of the first gantry, in front of the aircraft nose,
     the unit should then slide in through the 'Main Deck' loading door.

Neither idea worked and much discussion ensued. Ground Engineers suggested 'if we remove a cockpit window panel, the mast can be fed through cockpit, galley and into the Main Deck hold. It worked a dream.

The mast was safely stowed and all were happy. The B707 departed from

Gatwick and arrived Lagos on schedule. Off loading commencing shortly after the freighter was 'on stand'.

The loaders (porters) at Lagos tried every way they could think of to get the wretched mast out. Eventually, the Foreman Loader came up with the solution. He sent for a hacksaw and cut the mast into two equal parts.

Gatwick had, rather foolishly, forgotten to advise Lagos how they got it on and how, just as easily they could get it off in one piece!

INCOMPREHENSIBLE!

We, within the airline industry, have for many a long year believed that, incredibly, when you put an airline ticket into the average passenger's hand that you change his/her personality.

Numerous illustrations of this exists and here is one.

A lady in the Departure Lounge at Gatwick Airport, demanded in a perfect English accent, of the staff manning the Enquiries Counter:

"WHAT DOES (WAIT IN LOUNGE) MEAN?

The Passenger Services Agent sarcastically enquired:

"PRECISELY WHICH WORD ARE YOU HAVING DIFFICULTY WITH MADAM?" See what I mean? I guess it must be the unfound fear of flying.

THE CONTROLS

Airport controls are amongst the most secure in the transportation industry. They are by no means perfect.

A Baggage Facilities Agent on duty in the Customs Hall at Gatwick one mid morning, was confronted by an elderly lady, who in a broad cockney asked *"Ware the els me bleeding flight then?* Thinking that she was a rather tired arriving passenger, the Agent assured her that her baggage would arrive shortly on a designated 'Track'. *"Ah don't want me bleedin baggage, ah want me bleedin flight"* she insisted. "Where have you come from madam?" the Agent enquired.

"*Stepney, lived there all me life*" she moaned. "No, no madam, from where have you just flown in?" he went on.

"*I aint flowed in from nowhere, I wants to fly out. I'm going to Alicantee wiv me son and is family. We were all together in the Duty shop an we got separated, where the ell are they?*"

It was discovered, that somehow, the dear old soul had become separated from her family at the Duty Free Shop located at the end of the 'Terminal Finger'.

She passed arriving immigration, security and other 'fool proof' checks arriving in the Baggage Claim area, whilst she should have been at the Departure Gate.

Swift arrangements were made to advise the Gate that they not only had their missing passenger but that she was on her way by electric buggy to them.

ARMOURED CAR

In the 1960's, I was Alitalia's Sales Manager East Africa based in Nairobi. The outposts of my 'patch' were Aden and Sanaa in Yemen. At that time, the British were in control of Aden and not at all popular. Ironically in the early 1990's it was strongly rumoured that they had been invited back to help sort out the terrible economy! However, when not so welcome, there were some appalling terrorist activities against them. One very *'pleasant'* activity, was for assasins literally to shoot their victims in the back of the head as they walked past them.

In addition to the very special insurance cover that the company arranged, I courted the British Army in Aden. These super chaps ran frequent but irregular patrols around Aden. They agreed to take me with them, to enable me make calls on my Travel Agents, Commercial Houses and Government Offices but at specific times.

They would stop, literally for a few seconds to drop me off or pick me up. If I was not ready, they would not wait and I would have to find my own way back to my hotel. You can be absolutely certain, I was always ready. Mind you it cost me numerous bruises and scratches to my shins, hurriedly climbing into their Armoured Cars. I often wonder, if I was the only airline (or other) salesman to make his calls by such transport!

It was the only time in my 35 years of selling, that I ever told a client "At a given time, finished or not, I have to take leave of you". All completely understood. One of the most irritating and as a consequence, costly faults of any salesman is outstaying his welcome. I was always exceptionally conscious of this. Never, I hope, did any of my regular calls think, "Oh god, it's that bloody (airline) salesman again" I was told of numerous such thoughts about certain competitors.

On one call to an extremely hard working husband and wife (Ken and Rene Cunningham) owned travel agency in Chingola Zambia called 'International Travel Bureau', I got up 3 times to leave, having up dated them on my company's latest news and sales opportunities. Ken eventually said "Young Denis, what is the matter with you today. You are up and down like a yoyo?" I explained "When I had initially finished my call and got up to leave, Rene asked a question on another subject. I sat down and helped her. as I got up to leave again, you raised another point. I sat down again. I am prepared to sit and discuss business with any productive agent such as you, just as long as you require me. I never want to be considered a nuisance or worse be asked to leave". Ken assured me, that while he had thrown out many such pests, surely the revenue they (Ken & Rene) provided my company, proved, that would never happen to me. I was sincerely flattered.

On a call I made in the British Midlands, I was told, that the M.D was too busy to see me. I asked for three minutes to give him some important information and was shown in. I got up to leave after 2m 58 seconds. The M.D asked "And where are you going?" After explaining, I was invited to sit down, coffee was brought and after 42 minutes, I emerged with a group of 6 Business Class round trips, London–New York.

 # WORLD'S most TRAVELLED RAT

Air India International's (A.I.I) entire system was badly disrupted in the early nineties due to a rat having been discovered 'joy riding' their world wide network. As if the disruption to A.I.I and its passengers was not enough, the incident was the cause of a furore in the Indian Parliament. The furore was, because of that section of the Indian community who revere the rat as the mount of the Elephant God Ganesh not wanting the rat destroyed, whereas others did.

Those against the rats, did not stop with the aircraft of A.I.I, they wanted the pests eliminated from Indira Ghandi International airport and the Domestic

Airports of Bombay, as well as Delhi, Calcutta etc, you name it.

"MOST TRAVELLED RAT"

The incident began with a 12 hour delay at Kennedy New York, when an engineer 'on walk around', aircraft inspection, noticed the rodent through an open cargo hold door. An extensive search was mounted of the B747. All to no avail.

In Bombay, a further search was made causing the 747 to run 48 hours behind schedule. With commercial aircraft planned to operate fairly tight schedules (which most often they do quite well) the delay disrupted the entire A.I.I B747 fleet.

Whilst the concern over hygienic problems is grave, having such rodent(s) riding the holds of aircraft for long periods, has far greater risks than those of hygiene.

They have been known to gnaw their way through control cables, which could bring down an aircraft in flight. This actually happened to at least 2 African aircraft which crashed and which the investigative teams concluded were: 'RAT STRIKES'

The 'political' outcome, in India, was for parliament to authorise A.I.I to carry out a most extensive programme of trapping and fumigation.

FOOTNOTE

Air India, to my personal knowledge and satisfaction, having flown in excess of 75,000 miles with them, is a very good airline, very conscious of safety procedures. The rat(s) could have got aboard *at any one* of the stations on its worldwide network. Control of such problems is largely outside their authority. *Refer to* **THE GIANT COCKROACH** Page 44.

PROUD DIPLOMAT

One of the Counsellors at a western embassy in Freetown, Sierra Leone, was extremely proud of his new 'Audi' motor car. It had a built in computer, which literally told him by voice simulation of the need for service or if a fault had developed.

No longer would the garage get away with shoddy workmanship. If they failed to carry out repairs, or their work was not up to standard, the car would say so.

When he put his car in for service, he handed in a list of faults needing attention. When he got the car back, in spite of being charged for rectifying all, when he activated the computer, it advised him of where faults still existed. Thinking himself very clever indeed, he returned to his garage telling them where they were wrong. The garage foreman kept the car and set the mechanics to work immediately.

Again our man collected his car and again it told him of the shortcomings. Furious, he returned the car and remonstrated with the Service Manager, who assured him that he would be satisfied when he next collected his car. After collecting his car the third time, when he activated the computer, it remained silent. The diplomat was delighted and boastful in the Golf Club that evening. He was over the moon at beating the garage. A very suspicious club member asked to inspect the wonderful 'Audi' after the examination he proclaimed:

"As I thought, they have slit the throat of your famous computer!!"

 # CONFUSED

An Emirates Air Hostess, bought two beautiful Chinese dolls in traditional costume in Hong Kong, and displayed them in the lounge of her apartment in Dubai.

During a party at the apartment, two male colleagues *'stole'* the dolls for a gag. They fully intended to return the dolls in a few days.

However, when in Bangkok on 'layover' the male thieves decided to send a Post Card from the dolls. It related a host of excursions and romantic happenings of their visit. This prank was repeated from a variety of stations on the Emirates network. Convinced that the *'thief'* was an Emirates colleague, she was thrown off scent when cards arrived from non Emirates destinations. The *'thieves'* having asked colleagues in other carriers to send cards. They came literally from all over the world

The poor girl was totally confused, now believing that it was a non Emirates guest at her party who had stolen her precious dolls.

Eventually the dolls 'found their way home' to Dubai and looking not the least tired or worn they were united with their doting owner.

Never told what exactly had happened, or who was guilty, she was left to try to work it out for herself. If she reads this, her problem is solved.

'FRENCHIE'

Most of the South Terminal Departure Gates at London's Gatwick Airport were smiling one very busy afternoon in August '94.

A temporary French Passenger Services Agent, working with the major Handling Agent, was heard to say over the Public Address System which linked into ALL areas in that part of the terminal because the flight she was handling was delayed."LADIES & JENTLEMEN travelling wiv *Acme* Flight *abc* to *xyz*, pleeze urry up to Gate sirty sree to geet verified, because ah ave a very tight slot".

For the uninitiated : She was calling the departure of a delayed flight, suddenly allocated a departure time, made vacant by another carrier having a delayed flight. She was trying to say

"LADIES and GENTLEMEN, may I have your attention please. Would passengers travelling on Acme Flight abc to xyz, please report immediately to Gate 33, for passport verification prior to boarding. Your flight has just been allocated a departure time in 20 minutes. Thank you for your kind cooperation.

CHEEKY

On board a B.C.A.L B707 flying Freetown, Banjul London, was an 8 year old 'cheeky' unaccompanied minor.

When the 'Bar Trolley' reached his aisle, he was asked by a young stewardess, "And what would you like to drink before your dinner young man?"

"A Gin & Tonic ice and lemon slice" the impudent youngster replied. "Do you want to get me into trouble?" the stewardess admonished him.

In a flash, the youngster responded
"Sure, but only after I have had that G & T".

THE MODEL 'T'

With East African Airways in the mid 50's, I had a colleague Aziz Abdul Tejpar a prominent member of the Aga Khan led Ismaili community.

Aziz was a very keen supporter of the gruelling East African Safari Rally. From Good Friday to Easter Monday every year, with only one full 12 hour rest period, the rally travels some 2,000 miles (3,200 km) over some of the roughest roads in the world.

His love of cars, made him very elated one afternoon, when he came into my office saying "Denis. come quickly and see my new car". Parked outside our office in the McMillan Building in front of the New Stanley Hotel was a Model 'T' Ford. "New car" I exclaimed.
"Yes, yes, climb in" Aziz said excitely.

As we drove around Nairobi, I was given a 'lesson' on the rather different controls. Arriving back at the office. I expressed my understanding of his excitement at owning such a super car, but should it not be on show at his home?"

Aziz insisted that we change places and I drive the same route around the capital. However, this time, we will count the number of friends who wave to us. When we get back, I will borrow Abdul Gafoor Shiekh's Drop Head Chevey (Black with White & Lemon trim, the seats were of white leather), the very latest 'passion wagon' to arrive in Nairobi and drive the same route again counting the number of wavers.

Aziz was absolutely correct. It seemed as if all Nairobi was waving to us in the 'T', whereas in the beautiful 'Chevey' we only counted four!

"Now you see how much more attractive is my *new* Model 'T'".

WOULD THE PASSENGER WHO...

When on a flight from Dakar to Freetown, the Public Address system came to life with the following:

'WOULD THE PASSENGER WHO THOUGHT HE WAS DISEMBARKING AT ROBERTSFIELD MONROVIA, PLEASE MAKE HIMSELF KNOWN TO A MEMBER

OF THE CABIN STAFF. THIS AIRCRAFT IS OPERATING NON-STOP FREETOWN ABDIJAN'.

The poor man sitting across the aisle from me, protested vehemently about this 'late hour' of their decision. The cabin staff lied, that many announcements about the decision were made in the departure lounge at Dakar Airport.

Everyone within hearing supported the unfortunate passenger's argument but to no avail.

The crew's attitude was that it was the passenger's fault,'tough'!

1,200 MISHANDLED BAGS

In mid '94 at Gatwick Airport London, a most incredible 'cock-up' occurred. Two 'Big Busses' A300-600s were on the Satellite some 5 Gates apart. One was destined Rimmini on the Adriatic coast, the other South Tenerife in the Canary Islands. Their scheduled departure times were 10 minutes apart.

Although both flights were full, around 600 passengers in total, the boarding of each was quite smooth and uneventful, in spite of the close Gate proximity. Not until the Rimmini aircraft arrived, did the troubles start. As the baggage came into the 'Reclaim Area' not one of the flight's passengers claimed anything. Soon, it was realised, that the wrong baggage had been loaded and their bags were on another flight or were left behind. Problem was, the self same thing was thought in South Tenerife.

For some inexplicable reason, no less than 15 staff at Gatwick had 'screwed up'. One can understand how one, even two baggage containers can become mixed and loaded on to the wrong aircraft but eight mixed up was beyond belief.

The straight forward but not a workable solution, was for a cargo charter to operate Rimmini, Tenerife, Rimmini, simply because no aircraft was available.

There was not even a cargo charter available in the U.K to help out! The only, very expensive solution was for the airline to cancel two of its scheduled services and operate empty London Rimmini, collect the Tenerife baggage and fly there. Then reverse the operation and eventually fly Rimmini–London empty!

With the holiday resorts principal services being charters, such aircraft could not hope to lift an additional 600 bags for London and again get those bags to their correct destination.

The cost does not bear thinking about.

"TIME YOU SENT THAT DEPARTURE MESSAGE, MR. CHRISTIAN!"

'JOEY'

British European's 'Load Control' (The office in which all weight and balance calculations were carried, 'Load sheets' completed and 'Ships Papers' compiled General Declarations, manifests etc,etc, were placed into a concertina type bag (for down route stations) was located underground at London's Heathrow Airport, in the late 1950's.

Their staff were given a Budgie chick, unclaimed by an incoming passenger. In fact, one of their staff overheard a conversation of concern and he volunteered his section to care for the bird. They named it 'Joey'.

A member of 'Load Control' staff, wrote a 'Bulletin' on the incident and sent copies to all B.E.A route stations via the 'Ship's Papers' bags. Being very well received, a series of 'Bulletins' were dispatched regularly telling of 'Joey's' progress. It reported on his diet, his drinking habits, feather growth and change of colour as the bird matured, his singing and talking as his vocabulary developed.

Eventually it was decided to help him learn to fly. After all he was in an airline! This exciting news was well documented and disseminated to all very interested stations.

Suddenly, tragedy struck. On one of 'Joey's' flying expeditions. while on 'short finals' to a selected landing point, he flew straight into a plate glass divider and broke his neck.

An 'obituary bulletin was immediately dispatched. Cards, letters and even flowers of sympathy flooded in to 'Load Control' almost by return. It was decided to hold a funeral service and yet another 'bulletin' was actioned giving details of the date, time and place.

As a coffin, they used an old Havana Cigar box with all the advertising both paper and burnt on being removed. The 'coffin' was then polished and varnished.

At the funeral, every member of 'Load Control' staff both on and off duty were joined by all colleagues from operational sections at the airport. The *importance'* of the occasion was endorsed by the attendance of a representative of every foreign airline that B.E.A handled at Heathrow!

The 'Funeral' caused a 30 minute delay to all flights scheduled to depart at that time. B.E.A's hierarchy were very concerned. They were contemplating calling in a psychiatrist, frankly most non 'Load Control' staff thought their *Underground* colleagues were a trifle strange. When senior staff learned that a motif had been carved into the brick work over the grave, a positive decision was made.

With thanks to Graham Stephenson formerly of B.E.A/BA.

A WELL BALANCED AUSSIE PILOT

QUESTION
Describe a well balanced Australian pilot?

ANSWER
He has a 'chip' on BOTH shoulders!

FEMALE A.T CONTROLLER

A very charming Lady Air Traffic Controller in England who deserved much better, innocently enquired of a 'Brymon' Flight.
"Would you accept a turn on (To approach) at 4 miles?" Before Brymon could reply, Another aircraft in the zone responded "Lady, if he will not, I most certainly will and in any position!"

 ## A COSTLY LEG PULL

After a rather 'heavy ' but certainly not reportable landing by an extremely young, new First Officer, his very Senior Captain lifted the 'mic' and said:

"LADIES & GENTLEMEN, I must apologise most sincerely for that terrible landing. However, I trust that you will understand that it was by my very new and relatively speaking inexperienced First Officer. Whilst one has to make allowances for the 'new lads', that landing was just about the worst I have experienced in 40 years of commercial flying. I trust you will forgive him!

The enraged First Officer grabbed the 'mic' as the captain returned it to its holder, saying 'LADIES & GENTLEMEN. The indiscretion of the Captain was totally unjustified, I doubt if many of you even noticed, let alone felt any bump. I must say, that in all my 7 months commercial flying, I have never known such a bombastic, self opinionated, supersillious clown as this".

The Captain turned to his First Officer saying "You prat, you stupid idiot, I did not switch on the 'mic', I was just pulling your leg".

Disciplinary action resulted from the gaff, the Captain was reprimanded for his stupidity.

"......AND THE AUTOMATIC CLERK IS LABELLING THE PASSENGERS AND TELLING THE LUGGAGE TO BOARD THE AIRCRAFT."

AUTOMATED CHECK-IN

It is 0430 at Gatwick Airport London during the mid 70's. A queue has formed in front of the desk assigned to check in the first departure, a Brittannia Airways flight to Mahon.

Two young male passengers in their mid 20's, are leaning on the desk chatting. Unknown to them, the rather strange looking upright telephone in front of them, has been 'primed' to act as a loud speaker. The staff operating it, are one floor above, watching the 'Check In' desks.

Suddenly a **Dr Who 'DARLEK'** voice says *"Good morning gentlemen. This is a new automated Check In facility"*. The two passengers are visibly shaken. Initially they have no idea from whence the voice is coming.

DARLEK voice. *"Kindly place your tickets, open and upside down on the desk in front of you"*. The passengers comply.

DARLEK voice. *"Now your passports please"*. One passenger places his passport on the shelf he has been leaning on, immediately in front of him.

DARLEK voice. *"No, not there SIR, alongside your ticket please"*. The two men look over and around the desk but find no one.

DARLEK voice "Now gentlemen, place your bags on the scales please". The passengers comply.

The **DARLEK** shouts:

"EXCESS, EXCESS - OVERWEIGHT OVERWEIGHT, OFF LOAD, OFF LOAD THE PASSENGERS, THIS IS A CHARTER, THIS IS A CHARTER, NO EXCESS ALLOWED.

The poor passengers are distraught, with no one in sight to whom they can appeal.

After a few minutes the joke is revealed.

EXCESSIVE VIBRATION

Back in the days of 'compound engines', i.e. non turbo's, engineering both Flight and Ground would sometimes snag an aircraft for 'excessive vibration'. It occurred when, they could not synchronise the engines, or if an engine was not running smoothly.

A supervisor colleague in B.E.A, when asked the whereabouts of any given female, would say, with the straightest of faces.

"Oh she has been snagged for excessive vibration".

'AIRCRAFT CARRIER'

Male' International Airport in the Maldives, south west of Sri Lanka, was built across three islands between which the land was reclaimed. It is affectionately known as:

'THE LARGEST *PERMANENTLY* MOORED AIRCRAFT CARRIER IN THE WORLD'

The longest Helicopter scheduled service route network in the world is Hummingbird Helicopters Male', who pioneered their rota-wing inter island operations.

Their claim, is based on their 70+ flights per day, every day. As a tribute to their work, we include the cartoon.

OF COURSE IT'S 'MALE'. IT'S ONLY GOT ONE RUNWAY!

IN FLIGHT MOVIES

As the lunch service on board a B747 crossing the North Atlantic was being cleared away, the Flight Service Director announced over the Public Address.

"LADIES & GENTLEMEN, We are about to screen the movie. It is described as a 'Romantic Story'. Currently, we are passing over Iceland, where it is the mating season of the Polar Bears. Having seen the movie, I will make a point of keeping an eye open for some action down there on the ice. If I spot anything, I will most certainly let you know. It will, I can assure you, be far more interesting than that which we are about to project".

DUTY FREES

On board a British Caledonian DC10 flying from London to Rio, a lady in First Class was placing her Duty Free Order.

The last item she requested, was a large can of Caspian Caviar. Surprised, the Stewardess serving her advised that they did not have Caviar amongst their Duty Free items.

"Rubbish, you sold me a can on my way over to London 8 weeks ago, you are reserving it for someone down the back, now get me a can right away", the passenger demanded.

The stewardess tried in vain to convince her passenger. Eventually she excused herself and reported to her Purser, who one last time tried to explain that in his 15 years with the company, they had never sold Caviar. Recognising that it was futile to continue trying to convince her, he asked to see her ticket. and requested her address. he wanted to ascertain the North bound Flight number and Date for Customer Relations to write officially endorsing his statement. Madam, it would help our inquiries, if you could remember the basic colour of the tartan, the stewardess who served you wore. he queried. "Oh that's very easy, I recall it clearly. She described what her server had worn very clearly.

" Madam. I'm sincerely sorry to disagree with you, but we do not have those colours amongst our female colleagues uniforms. Are you certain that you flew B.C.A.L from RIO?"

The Purser had his suspicions that she had flown with another airline, in spite of her reservation on BR664 "Oh, I am naughty, my flight from Brasilia was badly delayed, I missed your flight at Rio. Your staff rebooked me on XYZ to abc where I had to make a connection to London. I am very sorry".

The Purser said "Madam should have thought of that earlier because your allegations could have wrongly got some innocent staff into a great deal of trouble. I was suspicious that you might have changed flights because there have been a number of rumours lately of the carrier you flew with, not serving the complimentary Caviar with the meal and selling it.

FEAR of FLYING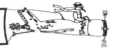

A lovely young woman, with whom I was in conversation, expressed her great fear of flying. She went on to remind me, that I some months earlier helped her overcome her fear and recommended she consider the U.S.A which could be less expensive than a European Holiday,

She told all assembled, that all she could cope with, was a flight to Spain. Remonstrating, I pointed out that air travel was the safest method of travel, illustrating my point with the current very high frequency in which commercial aircraft take off all over the world. I went on to say, that a take off to and landing In Spain, was no different to a flight to say Miami or Los Angeles.

"Oh yes it is" she said forcefully. "You see, I gather up all my courage to get on the aeroplane. Once on, I never look out the window and pray for a safe landing".
"OK, but I reiterate, once airborne to say Orlando, you still have only the one landing ahead of you". She came back with, "That is NOT the only problem. I cannot get up the courage to visit the toilet. Since I CAN hold out for three hours, there is no way I could hold out for nine or ten hours!!"

 # THE DINNER PARTY

An airline manager who served on a number of stations in Africa had acquired a wonderfully talkative African Grey parrot, was giving an important Dinner Party.

His principal guests were a husband and wife who adored that type of parrot. They asked for the bird to be allowed to sit on his self standing perch in the dinning room, hoping that it would as usual entertain them. They were not to be disappointed!

The host reluctantly agreed, because the parrot had contracted a heavy bout of flatulence. However, since his principal guests had requested it, he agreed. but first took the bird out to the garage, where he plugged the offending orifice with wax.

The first two courses went fine and the parrot remained silent. The main course was suckling pig, which was highly praised by all. Totally without warning, the parrot said:

"Lucky little suckling pig, lucky little swine.
You've got sage and onion up your arse,
I've got sealing wax up mine".

RFZ

In the Marketing Department of a major Islamic carrier in the Middle East, I saw the above sign in large letters over the coffee and tea making area.

Enquiring as to its meaning, I was asked "Which season are we in?"

We are in the Holy Month of Ramadan" I replied. This is the period when Muslims are expected to fast from dawn to dusk. During these long hours, when the heat can be intense, devout adherents are not allowed to eat or drink (some will not even swallow their own saliva).

Incidentally, the 'feast' moves forward every year about 21 days at a time. At least for the next six years, Muslims of the Middle East will fast during the cooler periods of the year. It dawned on me!

R.F.Z meant "RAMADAN FREE ZONE"! where many Muslim staff surreptitiously took their beverage with their non Muslim colleagues.

TIME

I understand, that behind the door of one senior executive of a major aircraft manufacturer, is a large sign which reads:

"IN SAUDI ARABIA, EVERYTHING EITHER TAKES 100 YEARS OR 10 SECONDS. IN THE MALDIVES, IT ALWAYS TAKES 100 YEARS!

COMMITTEES

SOME SOUND ADVICE.

A committee of one	GETS THINGS *DONE.*
A committee of two	FINDS THINGS *TO DO.*
A committee of three	WILL *WAIT AND SEE.*
A committee of four	*DELIBERATES MORE.*
A committee of five	WILL *CONTRIVE.*
A committee of six	WILL *OFTEN FIX.*
A committee of seven	*ISN'T HEAVEN.*
A committee of eight	*WILL DEBATE.*
A committee of nine	ALWAYS *WASTES TIME.*
A committee of more	IS AN *ENDLESS BORE.*

Don't you agree?

"E****H"

When aircraft request clearances from Air Traffic Control authorities, they are required to confirm verbally certain information. e.g. Total number of souls on board (T.o.B), Destination, Estimated Flight time, Quantity of fuel on board (endurance time), etc, etc.

In the Maldives, where the number of fixed wing aircraft movements is relatively very small, their exceedingly young Air Traffic Controllers, would benefit from appreciable increase in frequency of operations. N.B The average age of all staff working at Hule Hule Male' airport is only 22 years! Another problem, is their, in general, very limited knowledge of English, International Civil Aviation's chosen language of communication.

Most radio contact is, whilst understandable, restricted to set questions and phrases. This, as one can imagine tends to become somewhat irritating and frustrating to experienced expatriate pilots.

One American, who has since left "Because I can take no more of their nonsense" was a Captain with a local operator.

One day, he had all he could take of a particularly thick Air Traffic

Controller. Having twice provided the required answers to all the clearance questions, he was asked a third time "Quantity of fuel?" The irate captain was heard to respond in an extremely gruff and sarcastic voice, "E N O U G H!" as the Twin Otter shot across the lagoon on take off.

INQUISITIVE

In the First Class cabin of an Emirates flight from Hong Kong to Dubai, was a very drunk but trouble free businessman.

Amongst the Cabin attendants caring for the passengers, was an exceedingly voluptuous young female.

Pinned to her blouse, over her left breast was her name tag which read:
EMIRATES Felicity.

As Felicity leaned over our drunk in an aisle seat, to serve the passenger sitting in the window seat, the drunk, in a very slurred voice, whilst pointing at her right breast asked:
'Wa's the right one called then?

DEFIANCE

With British European Airways in the early 50's, we had a particularly bad disruption of services. fog was causing diversions all over Europe.

As the 'lowest thing' in Passenger Services, I was designated to take care of a group of nine Unaccompanied minors (UNMINS).

They were to depart on three scheduled flights spread over 47 minutes, however the first was not re scheduled to leave until after an additional 45 minutes had elapsed. Believing that the best thing to do as to keep the youngsters occupied, I asked the manager of the Bookshop/Newsagent, if I could bring them into his store and let them read comics. He kindly agreed. I planned to shepherd them out as their respective flights were called. After a toilet visit, I warned them that if they attempted to do a 'disappearing act' they were taking *their lives into their own hands!* No excuse *whatsoever* would be accepted for leaving the shop.

Literally, as I got them settled, my station Superintendent Willie Hall, on whose uniform were a total of eight gleaming gold rings and two stars was heard to say "Ah Long, I need you to do the following for me".

I explained my current special duties, adding that I was unable to leave them. "No problem, I'll take over because I have to be in the Departures Hall and what I require you to do takes you upstairs" said Willie. I took off as instructed. Who was I to argue with the station boss.

My new chore, took me within five minutes of the departure of the first three UNMINS. As I came up behind the children, I could hear them courteously but firmly informing Willie that all of his sleeve decorations did not impress them, he was NOT the gentleman who had instructed them:

a) To remain within the Bookshop
b) That **he** would personally collect them.

Willie was pleading with them (he having not noticed my return) but they remained defiant. As I came into view, ignoring my 'supremo' they were all asking *me,* "Are we ready to leave SIR?!"

QUESTIONS?

Those of us who have suffered the ravages of continental Air Traffic Controllers either 'Working to Rule' or worse still are on 'Wild Cat' strikes, will appreciate how very much time d-r-a-g-s. Over those long hours of waiting for news on the Estimated Time of Departure of their flight, passengers loose 'sight' of the time between going to the Enquiry Desk to ask yet again.

"Where is our aircraft right now? or When are we expected to leave?" etc.

Strangely, distraught passengers in such situations tend to ask the same questions over and over again.

One exhausted Passenger Services Agent, had, over the past 60 minutes, answered the identical question no less than 7 times of *the same family* head.

On his eighth visit to her desk in the 65th minute, the Passenger Services Agent got in first. "Tell me sir, how many are there in your party?"
"Five, my wife, three sons and I" she was informed.

"And what ages are your sons?" the P.S.A enquired.

"They are five, seven, and 11, no 12 well almost" the parent advised.

"Fine, go fetch your 12 year old son and I will tell him one more time, precisely what the situation not only is, but has been for the past three hours. He will I am certain, be able to retain this for much longer than you appear to have done"

The parent did exactly as he was instructed without any word of protest!

A RADICAL CHANGE

Flying between Houston, Texas and Phoenix Arizona with Continental Airlines in 1983, the Captain gave us a route report with a temperature at destination.

He announced "The temperature in Phoenix Arizona is 120 degrees Fahrenheit.

About 40 minutes later, the Captain came on again over the Public Address. "We are about to commence our decent and approach into the 'SKY HARBOUR' (is that not a lovely name for an airport?), in Phoenix. There has been a radical change in the temperature in this delightful city". We all sighed with relief.

After a moment or two , the Captain continued " It is now 119 degrees!" he finished with a chuckle.

 # CREW CHANGES

Whilst it is of paramount importance to recognise that every employee has to give of their very best, it is the public contact staff who, in the majority of cases bring back or push away customers.

Many years ago, a friend in B.O.A.C told me of a letter received in their Customer Relations department from a Diplomatic Courier. A 'special breed' amongst the most constant of air travellers.

Our passenger flew Johannesburg London on the same aircraft via Salisbury, Nairobi, Khartoum and Rome. In those days only a Standard Class service, no First, Business or Tourist/Economy Classes.

His letter ran along the following lines.

"The service Johannesburg Nairobi was, without any argument whatsoever, the finest I have experienced in too many years to count.

The Nairobi Rome flights made British Rail 3RD Class seem luxurious. Rome London was neither good nor bad, simply mediocre.

Why must those who pay, suffer the ravages of crew changes, which I recognise must be made? Surely your staff can be made to understand that their passengers are not to be made to suffer because someone, not necessarily a passenger has upset them".

Having been 'married' to the airline passenger service industry for nearly 50 years, I know well how disruptive one individual in the team can be, be it cabin crew or a passenger service staff member.

Sad to report, is the all too frequent consequences of the menstrual cycle and rows with 'boy friends'. The opinion shared by honest female colleagues as well as males.

FOOTNOTE.
While airlines have used very tall passengers who are regulars in their advertisements, no one, to my knowledge has ever used a Diplomatic Courier, possibly the world's most experienced professional passengers. While they may not be allowed to endorse a given airline whilst employed, there is nothing to prevent their use immediately they retire.

SANDWICHES

In the 50's, when I.A.T.A exercised a great deal more control over airlines than today, the single 'Standard' class cabin was divided into two classes.

The superior class became known as FIRST CLASS, the inferior TOURIST CLASS, now ECONOMY/COACH CLASS.

Disagreement regularly took place between carriers over the agreed standard of service in Tourist Class. At an I.A.T.A conference, it was agreed that 'sandwiches' would form the basis of the main meal.

It soon emerged that S.A.S's interpretation of a sandwich, was their famous smorgasbord – the open faced 'meal' on a slice of bread which they were serving. Protests were made to S.A.S to follow the agreed line. S.A.S ignored these words. Two major carriers, threatened S.A.S, that unless they 'towed the line', they would officially report them to the I.A.T.A enforcement office as being in violation of the agreement. I.A.TA cautioned S.A.S, that they were clearly in violation of the spirit of the agreement and that unless they followed the agreement, they would be fined. The complainants, on hearing that S.A.S were persisting with the smorgasbord, called for 'enforcement'.

In due course, S.A.S were fined, it was alleged, US$25,000. A sizeable sum at that time.

A short time later, the complainants were 'informed' that S.A.S were still at it.

Again, they advised I.A.T.A and yet another fine was imposed and paid. It is alleged, that, not only did S.A.S make provision for the fines in its' advertising budget – where else could they get such world-wide publicity for their competitors recognised superior Economy Class Service, for such relatively paltry amounts? but that Scandinavian anonymously kept briefing their competitors on their *illegal* higher standards!

It became known as the **'SANDWICH WAR'.**

FOOTNOTE.
S.A.S – Scandinavian Airlines System, according to Norwegians 'An airline run by Swedes, for the benefit of Danes and paid for by Norwegians', which speaks SASPERANTO (not Esperanto). In fact, English was and I believe still is, the official language of the tri nation initiative.

Yet another *smart* PR move was by a carrier who gave its Travel agents the most expensive quality of accepted give-a-ways possible e.g. ashtrays of Waterford Crystal. Their opposition got to hear of it and warned them to withdraw these ridiculously expensive gifts and replace them with accepted quality. The carrier concerned did as instructed but when doing so, advised the Travel Agents that they were forced into the action by their competitors!

 # THE COW in the GALLEY

Riding a U.S. carrier, we were privileged to have our 'Staff Rebate Tickets' to up grade to First Class actioned.

When asked if we would like coffee after dinner, we were also asked how we would like it. I replied, "generous cream, no sugar please". The coffee arrived with just a smidgen of cream, I requested the stewardess for a respectable increase. Sitting in Row 1, the coffee was served direct from the galley, situated immediately in front of us.

Asked if I would like a second cup, I reminded the stewardess of my request for generous cream. The coffee arrived yet again with a whisper of cream floating on the top. Without thinking, I quipped, "What's wrong with the cow in the galley, is its cream output in bottom gear?" As I said the last seven words, I realised my error and apologised profusely. Fortunately, the cabin stewardess, on seeing my embarrassment laughed adding "Forget it sir, she really is the dizziest colleague we have".

CEREMONIAL DRESS

Relations with the an African government over their refusal to externalise British Caledonian's sales (certified as genuine) surplus after station running costs, were in a bad state. As B.C.A.L's G.M, I frequently had to advise Government Ministers of the impossible economics of trying to operate an airline, when the carrier's legitimate earnings were blocked and held at the Central Bank, but to no avail. During one particularly frustrating meeting, I informed the Minister of Finance and his team, "That airlines fly through air, not on air". Release of legitimate funds was an essential ingredient to the continued provision of air services.

I advised my Head Office that a visit by our Chairman was required, citing the action of one major airline who, firstly threatened another African nation with withdrawal of their services under similar circumstances. When they took positive action, it resulted in the immediate release of the U.S.$5.7million of blocked funds.

When Sir Adam Thomson agreed, I made all the necessary appointments, confirming them in writing which I delivered personally to the Secretary to the President's Office. Our chairman had to make numerous changes to his very busy diary to make his visit. Arriving by K.L.M Thursday afternoon for the Friday morning audience, he planned to leave Friday night. On the Wednesday, I called the Secretary to the President re confirming the meeting. All was, I was assured, OK. On the dot of 0915 Friday, Sir Adam, Ian Ritchie External Affairs Director, Bill Richardson Engineering Director and I reported to the Secretary to the President. Greeted courteously, we were shown to the V.I.P waiting room to await our 0930 audience.

The appointed time came and went, as did 1000 hours. Used to being kept waiting for appointments with top Africans, we decided to sit tight until 1015. This also passed without any sign of action, save for the regular head appearing around the door and closing of it without a word.

There was no attempt at either an apology or explanation. I went to the Secretary's Office courteously pointing out that my Chairman and Directors had arranged this visit in extremely heavy and demanding diaries. Further they will have flown many thousands of miles by the time they arrived home. Equally courteously, I was assured that they were aware of this, I was asked to request patience from my colleagues. I reported verbatim.

More heads kept appearing around the door but not a word was spoken. At 1100, I again went to the office, on this visit my words were, per force, somewhat stronger. The Secretary was clearly very uncomfortable.

He mumbled, shifting from one foot to another but said nothing. I advised, that my colleagues would have to return to London and very carefully consider the company's position. The consequences, I personally hated to contemplate. He pleaded with me, "You see Denis, I have a major problem. His Excellency is in XYZ (some 250 miles up country)!" Having known this before our arrival, quite what he thought he would do was beyond us. May be he wrongly thought that we would disappear without explanation. He pleaded for us to return next morning when he guaranteed that the president would be present and *on time*.

Naturally we agreed. As we trooped out of State House, led by an angry Sir Adam, a newly appointed ambassador to the country, in full diplomatic regalia was seen getting out of his car. Clearly he was expecting to 'present his credentials'. In an attempt to ease the tension in our group, I quipped "It cost me a fortune to hire the actor and outfit to ensure that you did not feel the only party so treated". Our Chairman grunted, Bill Richardson laughed. As the ambassador came towards us, I asked if I should advise him of the president's whereabouts? Our Chairman said in an authoritative voice "No, let him find out for himself!"

 # THE BAGGAGE CART

At the Departures Immigration Desk of London Gatwick Airport, a passenger presented his passport for examination.

The Immigration Officer, while clearing the passenger was fascinated at his pushing an empty Baggage Cart. He asked the passenger "Excuse me sir, but why are you pushing an empty cart?"

Initially the passenger's reaction, was to glare at the Immigration Officer as if he was off another planet. His quizzical glare changed to a startled expression of concern.

"My God he exclaimed, where's my baggage" Suddenly he realised that he had left three suitcases on the 'Security X-Ray Unit' some eight metres behind him.   He had to take his baggage down to the Gate, where he was on Stand By for a seat to Dallas/Fort Worth.

FORENAMES

In Europe, they are generally called Forenames, Christian Names, Prenoms etc, etc. In the U.S.A they always refer to FIRST names.

One American at the Departures Immigration Desk, was requested to move to the centre of the desk and complete an Embarkation Card.

The Immigration Officer was working particularly hard, it being the height of the season and he did not initially speak to a passenger who was standing there doing nothing except for rubbing his chin. Eventually the Immigration Officer asked "Do you have a problem?"

"Sure do, your card asks me to write my forenames and I only have three!"

 ## 'TECH' DELAY

How often have you heard, at an airport "We have a tech(nical) delay. Further information will be given in one hour" or something similar.

Not, I will wager, anything like as frequently as in the days when aircraft powered by compound engines flew the worlds' routes. Back in the late sixties, it was quite a common occurrence. With the introduction of the jet engine, the number of moving parts in an aircraft engine was cut almost in half. This miracle of engineering reduced the delay factor by an even bigger percentage.

A total compound engine change, was an accepted, albeit reluctantly, occurrence. For a number of years, at Ciampino (Rome) Airport, we had an

Argonaut Engine which had been flown out as a replacement unit. While awaiting its arrival, the Station Engineers had fixed the 'sick engine' and the delayed service departed. Someone suggested that the 'spare' be returned to base a.s.a.p but a sensible engineer suggested 'Wait until they call for it'. They never did and it was used as a 'private' spares facility for a very long time. It became known as *'Smith's* engine'.

One of the most infuriating 'tech' delays, is the 'creeping delay'. It occurs when the engineers are not at all certain of what the problems is. They spend hours trying one cure after another. As each turns out to be incorrect, they add another hour or so to try another cure. Although somewhat more technically advanced, it is similar to the motor-car engine, except the aircraft engineers never *think* they have it right.

Believe me, it is not done to inconvenience passengers, who always seem to think it is! The airline staff, are every bit as anxious to see you safely on your way, as you are. After one wretched 'creeping delay', 'ROY' produced the cartoon depicting how a Chinese airline solves its' problems.

"I'M NOT AGAINST ACUPUNCTURE, BUT I THINK THAT WE IN THE WEST WOULD CHANGE THE ENGINE!"

THE FLIGHT INSTRUCTOR

My son, now a qualified Multi Engine Commercial Pilot with Instrument Rating tells of a very powerful personality, a Flight Instructor in the U.S.A.

When Mark asked a long term student "What is Mr .... like?"

He was told "He is a kindly man, with fear on tap".

THE MACABRE SMUGGLER

A Cabin Attendant on an Air Canada London Toronto service was concerned, that a lady declined her repeated invitation to heat a bottle for her baby or accept her offer to nurse her baby during the eight hour flight.

Each time she offered her assistance, the lady reacted most strangely. The Cabin Attendant was so concerned that she mentioned it to her Flight Purser, who suggested that she report it to Toronto Customs. Neither had ever known a mother, with an infant, refuse *any* assistance.

From a discreet distance, the Cabin Attendant indicated to Customs which passenger she was concerned about.

The passenger was interrogated and it was discovered that her baby was dead! Customs were not only concerned, they were very suspicious, A doctor was called. On examination, he declared that the infant had been dead for in excess of 24 hours, Further examination horrified a Pathologist. The infant's body was packed with Heroin in plastic bags!

SEQUEL.

In December 1994, an English Sheep Dog, which had arrived at London from Bogota Colombia as cargo, was noticed to be unwell. Investigation revealed, that the poor animal had a large quantity of Heroin inside it in a plastic bag. After removal of the bag, the dog made a rapid and full recovery.

SEDIA GESTATORIA

In the fifties, a Catholic Priest and a Rabbi found themselves sitting next to each other on a transatlantic flight. They chatted most amicably. Just prior to lunch, a stewardess brought around the wine list and asked the Priest, "What would you like Father? The priest skimmed through the list, his eyes settling on his favourite tipple which he strongly recommended to his new found friend. He added "This wine is the favourite of the Holy Father". After tasting the wine, the Rabbi ordered two more bottles. Both enjoyed the wine so much, that the Father insisted on returning his companion's hospitality by ordering two more bottles.

A potent drink, the Rabbi quipped "I now know precisely why you carry your Holy Father around on a raised throne, on the shoulders of four bearers!"

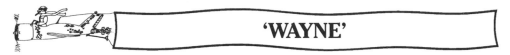

'WAYNE'

During the mid nineties, QANTAS (Australia) Flight Deck crews went through a somewhat traumatic time.

Said to behave as a very superior breed to their Cabin Crew colleagues(similar to their British counterparts of the fifties) they were rocked to their foundations, when a First Officer called WAYNE was caught in the B747/400 crew rest bed with not one but two stewardesses.

Some Australian pilots, disenchanted with Qantas, then working with a number of **non** Australian airlines, were putting the news of 'the shame' about at every possibility.

As a consequence, hundreds of pilots, on hearing a Qantas flight call up an Air Traffic Control centre world-wide, would 'click on' their 'RT' and ask "Wayne, is that you Wayne? in a wide mixture of pronounced accents.

Hindi	"My Gawd Vayne, is that you sahib?"
British	"I say old boy, is that you Wayne old chap?"
North American	"Gottcha Wayne ol' buddie"
Japanese	"Ah so, Wayne san Hi domo"
French	"Sava Wayne mon petit chue?"
German	"Gut morgan Her Vayne, alles gut yah?"

Even Air Traffic Controllers have been suspected of taunting Qantas, when acknowledging a call ie "Qantas XYZ requesting clearance to 25,000' " to hear "Wayne you are –" then because this is highly irregular, switch to "Qantas XYZ you are cleared to 25,000' ".

The problem for Qantas crews was, they had no way of knowing precisely which aircraft was responding to their calls.

THE OVERHEAD BIN

Circa 1992, when operating to Tehran, a Middle Eastern carrier had a strict company policy which dictated, that no member of the crew was to disembark from the aircraft during the 'turn around'. This was to prevent them from becoming 'commercial hostages'.

During one 'turn around' of a 'wide body' service at Teheran a steward was working, with a lady Flight Service Supervisor (F.S.S) whom he thought a great deal of. In spite of this, he very much enjoyed 'pulling her leg'.

On hearing that there was to be a delay of 45 minutes, giving them 2 hours on the ground. the steward pointedly asked the F.S.S, knowing full well the rules, if 'he could go ashore'. The F.S.S remonstrated with him, emphasising that he knew full well the company policy. He appeared to accept it and went into the cockpit, ostensibly for a chat with the captain. In fact, it was to brief the captain on what he was up to.

For the next 20 minutes, the steward studiously avoided the F.S.S and persuaded a fellow Cabin attendant to go to her and ask her "Where is XYZ? I have had not seen him for over 30 minutes and he said that he was going ashore".

The F.S.S who was eating her lunch in the empty First Class cabin, immediately stopped and thoroughly searched the entire cabin . No sign of her steward!

Furious, she went to the cockpit asking the skipper if he had seen *XYZ* in the past 45 minutes. He had, he replied, adding that the steward said he was 'going ashore'. The F.S.S was beside herself with worry. She was also very, very angry.

"Friendship Is all very well, but not only defying company rules but playing me off against the captain's authority was totally unacceptable. This time young XYZ had gone too far, I will report him in writing".

The other cabin staff managed to calm the F.S.S down and persuaded her to return to her salad lunch, manoeuvring her gently back to her vacated seat.

One got her an A4 sheet of paper and a pen to start drafting her report.
All of a sudden, the cover of the 'overhead bin', immediately over the F.S.S flew open and she heard her missing steward call her name'
She threatened instant death, when she could get her hands on him!

COMING THROUGH!

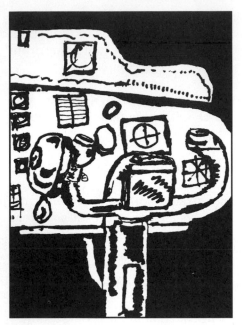

As an aid to pilots of a client airline with which it had recently signed a contract to supply a number of turbo-prop airliners, a prominent European aircraft constructor has had fitted to the 'yoke' of every aircraft in their customer's new fleet of aircraft, a very simple but effective warning system.

It is designed to inform all other aircraft on the ground and presumably in the air, that they are about to be passed or overtaken.

EVIDENCE LEFT! TAKEN FROM MANUFACTURERS MANUAL.

Note BICYCLE BELL. CLEARLY the responsibility of the FIRST OFFICER.

AN IRISH TAIL or TALE

A U.S.A carrier, at one time had a B707 which had a nasty habit of quivering in flight.

They heard that Aer Lingus (Ireland) were 'breaking up' a damaged B707. Believing that if they changed the 'vertical stabiliser', they could cure the problem with their aircraft.

They did a deal with Aer Lingus and shipped the unit to Dallas–Fort Worth. Here they changed the stabilisers over.
The U.S. carrier's aircraft flew superbly.

MORAL
"You can fix anything with a piece of Irish tail!!"

JET LAG

Flying either eastward or westward through time zones, affects passengers in different ways. For most of my career, I was exceptionally fortunate, in that it had little effect on me.

As late as my 52nd year I was able to fly Freetown to London to Los Angeles to Auckland N.Z, some 36 hours of continuous travelling. I then drove 400 miles from Auckland to Wellington. I *sincerely* did not feel particularly tired and since the chances of getting seats on N.Z. National Airways Auckland Wellington were non existent that morning and afternoon together with an good offer from Hertz, I decided to drive. After all, we required a car in Wellington. This is not related to announce any sort of achievement, one either has the gift or one does not.

Ten years later, after travelling Male' to Colombo, to Dubai, to London (overnight) and then London to Houston, to Phoenix. It took me 14 days to adjust, in time for the same journey in reverse!

What happened to a Businesswomen some years back warrants telling. After a Long Haul flight from London to the Far East, all she wanted to do, was to take a long hot bath and go to bed with a bottle of chilled white wine.

After taking her long hot bath, and towelling down, she, as in a dream, drifted out of the bathroom, through the dressing room and into her bedroom.

At least, that is what she thought! She had in fact, opened the wrong door, finding herself in the hotel corridor, stark naked and with no key to open the self locking door!!

As if this was not enough, a very boisterous group of men, attending a convention in the hotel, appeared from around the corner!!

THE NYMPHOMANIAC

A male passenger, on a B747 ten hour overnight flight, was awoken by a female Flight Attendant three hours before landing, who offered to have sex with him. During the last hour of the flight, this fellow, while chatting to a male Flight Attendant, boasted of his experience and of how *good* the girl was.

The Steward wise cracked, "Well, she ought to be, she is a nymphomaniac who 'lays' at least three men on a 10 hour night flight. In fact you were number five last night".

The subject male passenger's pride was so sorely hurt, that he wrote to the airline's Customer Service Department complaining of 'His feeling dirty at having been the fifth conquest *of this disgusting woman"*.

THE NIGHTMARE

There were three of us at Entebbe airport Uganda in the early seventies, discussing the B747. The conversation drifted around to a spate of technical problems, the *Type* was experiencing at that time. B.O.A.C was having its' share and we were wondering how many units they were currently operating.

Babu thought they had 14, Francis thought 11 and I said that I thought it closer to 17 adding why do we not ask BA's Station Engineer who had waved to us some 15 minutes earlier from across the tarmac.

He said that he was not exactly certain but knew it was between 15 and 18. What he did know for certain, was, he having just been speaking to Nairobi, was where nine of them were right now.
Fascinated we asked. 'Where are they?'.
All 9 are in Jomo Kenyatta Airport Nairobi'. he grinned.
a) Is in transit between London and Johannesburg.
b) Is in transit between London and Dar es Salaam.
c) Was on turnaround at Nairobi. Returning to London that night.
d) Yesterdays London Johannesburg was 'sick'.
e) Yesterdays Dar es Salaam London was 'sick'.
f) Was another 'sick' unit, diverted into Nairobi on a Salisbury London sector.
g, h and i) Had been sent out from London to 'rescue' the delayed passengers and one after the other, they had joined the 'sick' parade.

It was a Station Engineer's nightmare.
Thank God their performance has radically changed for the better

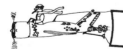 # PANIC

The Kissy Tagrin Ferry, which serves Freetown Airport from Freetown City, across the Sierra Leone river was loaded to the gunwales. There would have been around 30 cars plus approximately 100 occupants and 300 pedestrians on board.

Suddenly, a large Citroen motor car, smack in the middle, started to emit considerable amounts of smoke from all engine outlets.'Fire, Fire!', shouted those in the immediate vicinity.

Panic broke out, with passengers jumping overboard in their hurry to escape.

Whilst comic to observe, it was very tragic.

The ferry, was firmly tied up at Kissy Jetty and all that was required was an orderly walk off by all passengers.

GREED

On a Monday morning, as the B.M.W franchise holder opened his showroom, a young airline steward, walked in announcing his interest, in a most superior voice, in their top of range model with every available accessory, he having won the National Lottery.

The salesman hurriedly informed his Sales Manager who invited the young man into his office for coffee and croissant. The Sales Manager then demonstrated his most powerful sales pitch, extolling the virtues of 'his' Seven Series.

May I test drive it?" the Steward asked.
"Certainly SIR, we will do even better than that. If you will understand that our 'demo' model does not have all available accessories, we will loan you a Seven Series for a week with our compliments. Naturally, I will guide you through our comprehensive accessory catalogue". An hour later, our young hero was driving off with a full tank, a temporary fully comprehensive insurance certificate and a large bag of B.M.W 'goodies'.

On the following Monday morning, our 'winner' drove into the Mercedes Benz agency forecourt. He told the staff, of his win adding, that he was not 100% satisfied with the B.M.W. "May I test drive your 500SL?"

The M.B staff were every bit as enthusiastic as their competitors. Not only did they offer to match B.M.W's service, they offered to follow him back to the B.M.W forecourt and await him at a discreet distance.

At the end of the second week of the exercise, the 500SL was returned. The young man, while asking for a day or so to decide, expressed a few doubts .

A day or so later, the two Sales Managers were enjoying a 'Bar Lunch' in their local, they got chatting and realising that they had been duped, agreed jointly to prosecute.

In court, the Judge was extremely annoyed and very forthright.
"If you think, that I am going to countenance your greed, you are very wrong. This young man told you the truth, he did win the Lottery. The fact that you could not be bothered (in your greed) to check that it was only ten pounds, will teach you a lesson.

 # ENGERLICH

I heard, that in an office of Her Majesty's Government in Hong Kong, there have been thousands of examples of misuse of English in the writing of memos.

Two worthy of recording were sent to a Departmental Head were:

a) "We, the staff are velly concerned over security of our office. We believe, that it would be of need to have a button for the squeezing installed under the Cashier's draws".
b) "With jackets lying everywhere around in office, we need a good supply of *hookers,* especially at night".

30,000 FEET

Some years before Pan American went out of business, one of their B747 aircraft flying at 30,000' over the North Atlantic suffered a nasty shock.

Cruising high above the ocean, a very large Goose smashed through the cockpit window. It passed between the two pilots narrowly missing the Flight Engineer, impacting into the cockpit - cabin door.

It was later discovered, that geese climb to these great altitudes where, their wings stiffen and get close to freezing, the oil in their feathers protects them from actually freezing. It was also discovered, that the birds actually sleep on the wing, gliding on the 'Jet Stream' currents.

An inane young journalist attending a press conference on the incident, asked a respected Ornithologist "What he thought was the last thing on the goose's mind at the time of impact?"

The Ornithologist sarcastically replied.

"No doubt it was his backside!"

THE TRATTORIA

In a street in Florence, close to the church of Santa Maria d'Novella, is a Trattoria called either Sostanza or Constanza. I cannot recall which. It is possibly the best Trattoria in Italy. It certainly is the only one I have ever seen Italians queueing for.

We were there in 1963. Sitting at the raw wood tables, where waiters with a carpenter's pencil, will write up your meal with costs and then erase with sandpaper.

We were practicing how we would order our meat the way we prefer it cooked. I like it well done, my wife just done.

After 15 minutes or so, a local elderly gentleman with a beautifully groomed goatee beard and moustache, asked in perfect English, "Where are you from my children?"

We replied Zambia, formerly Northern Rhodesia".
You are putting together your requirements (in Italian) are excellent. Alas, all is in vain".
I responded with surprise, "Surely the waiter speaks Italian". N.B The dialect of one town in Italy, can be incomprehensible to a man in a town a mere 5 kms away.

"Oh yes, he speaks Italian, that is not the problem" said our new found friend. "What is then?" I quizzed.
"The problem is, that in this establishment, the chef decides how the meat *will* be cooked. If you do not like it that way, you are free to eat elsewhere!"

FINE!

On a visit to Singapore in 1993, I was impressed to see the progress made under the guidance of Senior Statesman Lee Quan Yew.

To achieve his goals of modernising and cleaning up the city he was forced to introduce some fairly draconian laws with stiff penalties. If caught wasting water, the penalty was S$200, for chewing gum S$150 and so on.

In the taxi from Changi International Airport to my friend Walter Riggans home, I chatted to the driver. "Many large and important changes have been introduced to Singapore. How do you find them?" I asked. *"FINE"* the cabby replied.

"Oh, you are happy with them then" I commented.

"I did not say that. I said *FINE* It's a *FINE* for this, a *FINE* for that, in fact its a *FINE* for every bloody thing" was the smiling cabbies response.

N.B A few years later, my friend and neighbour bought me the 'TEE SHIRT' Front shown below and back to the right.

THE CALL BUTTON

An Indian male passenger in Economy Class, trying to attract a Cabin Staff member's attention via the overhead call button, beckoned a passing steward. Indicating towards the button which has the internationally accepted design of a female on it, says

"I have been fingering lady for 30 minutes without any response".

"That sir is because, you are not practicing the *new* method of foreplay".

MY EPITAPH

In the late fifties my industry colleagues & friends used to tease me about the epitaph they would have on my 'head stone'. This was because of my approach to planning and costing long distance itineraries and fares. Based on my philosophy, they said the epitaph should be:

DRAW A LITTLE MAP
&
WHEN IN DOUBT CHARGE THE HIGHER AMOUNT

DRAW A LITTLE MAP.

I would take an A4 sheet and lay it horizontally. Then I would draw out the routing. This immediately gives one a very good idea of what fare should cover the majority, where to 'break' the fare and where side Round or Circle trips should/could be charged. This would ensure the best value for the passenger.

WHEN IN DOUBT CHARGE THE HIGHER AMOUNT on fares.

One can always refund an overcharge but trying to recover an under collection is virtually impossible.

Evidently I would always counsel and practice both.

Today, staff simply consult a computer.

THE WAKE UP CALL

We were at Colombo in transit for around 10 hours between London and Male' Maldives. Given a 'Day Room' at the Airport Garden Hotel by Air Lanka. We decided to sleep after the 18 hours travel since leaving home in England.

I put in a 'wake up call' for 1730, we having to leave the hotel at 1845. I set my wrist watch' alarm as a back up. On cue, my alarm buzzed. We set about our toilet duties preparing for the last sector.

Because no 'wake up' call came. I called the operator. "May I have a local time check please?"

"Precisely 1745" the operator advised.
"Great, what the hell happened to my wake up call of 1730?" I said in a very sarcastic and annoyed voice.

"I'm terribly sorry sir, there has been an unfortunate error" he said. At this point, I was happy to accept his apology but not the usual lame excuse or argument.

I remonstrated over the inconvenience of a possible missed flight.
The wretched operator was beside himself with apologies, finishing with "May I call you now sir?"

VEG or NON VEG?

In the Cabin Staff Training School the boys and girls are taught to ask every Economy Class passenger if they would prefer Chicken Makanwallah or Vegetarian cutlet.

Inevitably, this comes down to 'Veg or non veg?' when asking 235 passengers on a full Economy Class Flight to Bombay.
The all too familiar response by Asian passengers is "I am chicken, my vife is wegetable".

Some cabin staff are frequently heard to say,
"Yes sir, that is well known, but what would you care to eat?"

A CHINESE FIXATION

I understand, that Chinese males have a fixation over well endowed European women.

Back in the early sixties, a very young newly qualified B.O.A.C air hostess was on her first crew 'layover' in Hong Kong. In a large department store, a Chinese male said something to her which caused her some considerable distress.

As she exited the store, she bumped into her very jovial captain. Seeing she was clearly disturbed, he asked her what was wrong. Hesitantly, she said 'A very well dressed Chinese man approached me saying "I will give you U.S.$50 if you will let me feel your breasts" Shocked I ran out.

"Where, was it, in this store?" enquired the captain.

"Yes right here" she responded indignantly.

"Good, let's go back in, if we get all the males lined up, we can make enough to have a whale of a party when we get back to Karachi tomorrow night!"

VISUAL IDENTIFICATION

My wife Anne was working as an air hostess with B.O.A.C in the early fifties. On a Stratocruiser en route London New York, her landing position was a 'jump' seat between and behind the Captain and his First Officer.

In the zone over Gander Newfoundland, early one spring morning, she sat down and strapped herself in for landing. She became concerned at the cross talk between the two pilots.

With no head phones, Anne could not hear the Air Traffic Controller's side of the conversation. Her pilots side ran something like this:

Cpt There it is at 0200'.
F/O No – it's at 1000'.
Cpt Are you sure? I think it's at 0300 now.
F/O No, I feel certain that it is at 1100 now.

Anne thought, 'My God, even allowing for the scores of frozen lakes down there, I thought that they would have far more precise way of locating the snow covered runway'.

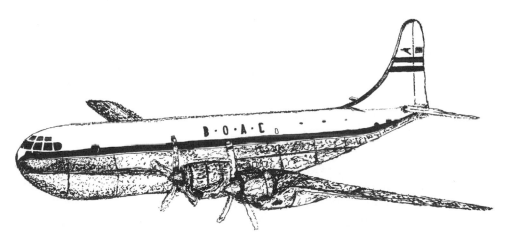

When they eventually landed, she queried the procedure with the First Officer, who laughed saying that they had been advised by A.T.C, that an R.C.A.F jet trainer was in the area and that his radio had become U/S (unserviceable).

They had to identify his position visually for their, as well as his safety.

 ## COMPANY IDENTIFICATION

As the company representative on an overseas station, we were briefed to obliterate all company identification on any of our aircraft involved in a crippling accident. Many other carriers, issued very similar instructions to their station number one.

An airline severely damaged a DC10 at Robertsfield Airport Liberia.

The company manager was most anxious to follow the company guide-line. He went out and bought a number of 4" wide rolls of gummed brown paper. The type one uses to seal cardboard boxes.

At the airport, he organised a gantry and six porters to help him carry out his instructions. The gantry was positioned close to the fuselage and the six covered the logo on the aircraft tail. They then very diligently stuck the brown paper over the letters of the company name.

Problem was, he had instructed the porters to attach the gummed paper over the actual painted letters, which did nothing to hide the company name. It merely changed the colour!

GYNAECOLOGIST

Shortly after taking up residence in our first permanent overseas posting, we became firm friends with a Gynaecologist.

One evening at dinner with a number of other friends, the conversation drifted round to the potential dangers of discussing ones work with anyone, other than the person(s) it concerned. Our 'gyne' friend told us of an incident which had caused him the most embarrassing moment of his life.

He had been attending the wife of a friend, who had been complaining of woman's pains. He prescribed medication, asking his patient to return after five days. With no improvement, he prescribed another form of treatment, with a request that she come back to see him in seven days.

On her third visit, the patient advised that the pain had become worse.

Our friend decided that the time had come for an internal examination. He found a condom, which he removed. Not wishing to embarrass his patient, he advised that a small obstruction was the cause of the problem which he had now removed.

Next day, the patient called saying that she felt fine.

A few days later, during a round of golf with the husband, our 'gyne' tactfully pointed out that his friend should be more careful after making love with his wife. Puzzled, the husband requested an explanation.

"Your lack of diligence, has caused Laura's painful discomfort".

Even more confused, the husband said that he had not the vaguest idea what his friend was talking about.

"Well, Laura's pain was as a result of a blockage caused by the condom you left behind".His friend's reaction was both instantaneous and angry.

"I have never used a condom in my life!"

THE CONTROL OFFICER

Attractive, tall, slim and about 35, she approached the Immigration Officer's Desk with her arm outstretched proffering her passport for examination.

As the Immigration Officer's hand took hold of the document, a look of considerable apprehension appeared on the woman's face. She made a vain attempt to retrieve the passport.

Apprehensive, the I.O turned the passport over to have the front cover uppermost. As he did so, two small condom packets fell onto his desk.

The passenger turned scarlet. As the I.O scooped up the packets discreetly returning them to his passenger he *whispered* 'No problem madam, I, madam, am a Passport Control officer, not a Birth Control Officer'.

The lady gratefully thanked him for his discretion, her male escort having neither heard nor noticed a thing.

THE DEPORTEE

Having come off duty as an Immigration Officer at 1400 hrs, I awaited the arrival at Gatwick of my wife who was going to Dublin to attend a residential course. She was travelling on a Subject to Space Staff Rebated ticket and I wanted to help get her baggage down to the Departure Gate.

Wearing my Airport 'ID', after registration, I escorted her to Security Control where I lifted her hold and hand baggage onto the X-Ray Unit.

My wife put her hand bag on herself. After passing through the X-Ray I returned her two heavy bags to the Baggage Cart and we walked down to Gate seven where we presented her Stand By Boarding Card..

In a very few minutes, my wife realised that I had not lifted her hand bag off the X-Ray Unit. I returned to the control to collect it.

On arrival there, I found the supervisor and one of his staff writing out a list of all the contents. I was told, that I would have to sign for it. I agreed.

After the usual wisecracks, they came to her passport. Initially, they queried her carrying such a document between London and Dublin. I explained that she was airline staff and that in the event of difficulty in getting a seat directly home, she could travel via an international route if necessary. As they came to writing the passenger's name, the supervisor said "But you are Mr Long, what a coincidence!"

Puzzled I queried the remark. "But are you not deporting the passenger" he asked. I explained why I was there.

After my wife was given a seat, I returned from the Gate, via Security where I advised them that "I kissed my deportee goodbye".

THE 'RUSSKIE'

When nationals of the former U.S.S.R depart from the U.K, they are required to complete an Embarkation Card.

One mid morning at Gatwick, an exceptionally well spoken young man wearing a boater, Eton jacket and tie came up to my desk with a beautiful young woman on his arm. He placed two passports in front of me. One C.S.S.P, the other British-European Community.

I said "I must ask for madam to complete an Embarkation Card please sir."

"Not necessary, you see, I'm the bloody Ruskie" the *apparent* young Englishman laughingly informed me!

THE REST ROOM

A veteran of American Commercial Aviation was close to retirement. Being of Irish decent, he had visited his ancestral home and with his wife decided that he would like to spend his summers in Ireland. They decided to invest in a cottage in the village from whence his grandparents originated.

Recommended to a property with a particularly beautiful view, owned by a gentleman with no one to leave it to, they made arrangements to view,

At the cottage they were surprised not to find a toilet in the house. They asked the owner "Where is your Rest Room?"

"Me what? said old 'Paddy'.
"Your W.C, your toilet" they said.
Ah, sure, tis at the bottom of the garden, just like all the houses around here".
That evening, 'Paddy' was in his local Pub and Mike said to him

"I hear you're about to sell the old place, how is it going?"

"Well, generally it's going quite well, but there is a very strange demand from the buyer, he wants a lock put on the bog door" said 'Paddy'.

"What's so strange about that?" asked Mike.
"Well, my family and I, have owned that place for almost a 100 years, in living memory, we have never had anyone steal a bucket of *shit* from there!"

 ## THREAT of WAR

We had 'checked-in' at Heathrow, for our flight with Air India to Delhi. I asked if any of our old East African Airways (Dar-es Salaam) friends, reported to have joined A.I.I were available.

We were told, that *Arson Fernandes,* formerly a Duty Officer in Dar, was in the Duty Officer's office, located at the far end of the 'Check-In' desks. We were invited to call in. As we neared the office, we could hear a heated argument.

On entering, we found staff of both Air India and Pakistan Airlines almost at each others throats 'discussing' the threat of war between the two 'sub continentals'.

"And just what do you think you are going to do if Pakistan does move in and take over Kashmir / Jamu?" said a cocky P.I.A Airport Manager.

Quick as a flash, his Air India counterpart retorted "We will bomb Bradford!" For the benefit of the uninitiated, Bradford is full of Pakistani Muslim immigrants.

 # STRONG HEAD WINDS

In late 1974, I had a small surplus of leave already carried over from 1973. I had to 'use it by the next March, or loose'. Although demands in the office had repeatedly been the cause of my delaying taking it, I had not actually had an application refused and so could hardly request a further extension.

With my wife tied to a strict teaching schedule, I decided to visit some friends and business contacts in San Francisco. T.W.A kindly gave me a free ticket, Space Available of course, because my travel was strictly personal.

At Heathrow, I, with a number of T.W.A staff, was at the Gate awaiting news of our 'fate'. Would we or would we not get onto the flight?

The flight captain appeared at the podium and told his ground colleagues "We have a forecast of strong 'head winds' and will have to call en route for fuel. I can uplift maximum weight here. Just as long as you have a vacant seat, I do not want anyone left behind and that includes staff". Splendid chap, we were all accepted.

The winds were even stronger than forecast, our captain decided to get into Bangor Main on the U.S. East coast and fuel up. During the flight from London, I had chatted to the Flight Service Director (FSD) a Chinese American with a most jovial disposition.

As we got close to Bangor, the captain advised that we would be the 14th unscheduled B747 to call at Bangor, 12 were still there, the terminal was overloaded. As a consequence we would have to remain on board during fuelling. Under such circumstances, all the aircraft doors MUST remain open, being winter, we were half frozen. The passengers were understanding and generally very good natured.

My *friend* the F.S.D came over and very quietly advised that "He and his staff were in for a *very bumpy ride* to San Francisco". Thinking it was weather, I casually enquired as to how they were going to handle the next meal service. "Oh its not that, the problem is that the 13 747 'diverts' ahead of us have *'drunk the joint dry'*. There literally is no alcohol available to us, or those coming in behind us. The airport stores and bar are empty, as are all the Liquor Stores in and around Bangor. Man, this is probably going to be the first B747 dry flight in U.S. history".

The understanding attitude of the 350 odd passengers markedly deteriorated.

WHAT A SAUCE!

On a duty visit to Buenos Aires in 1977 I was booked into a most prestigious hotel. At dinner, the first evening, I asked my waiter for the Worcester Sauce, a great compliment to Argentina's most excellent beef. To my surprise, he said that they had none but offered me a very poor substitute.

The next evening, while about to start my Main Course, I observed my waiter pushing a beautiful trolley past my table, laden with a fine selection of sauces. In front, most resplendent was a bottle of Worcestershire sauce. I asked the waiter to come to me, after he had finished his immediate chore.

When he returned, I quietly remonstrated with him over his statement of the previous evening, but he yet again denied having any Worcester Sauce. Lifting the Worcester Sauce bottle, I said What is this?"

"Oh *no* sir, that she is *SHAKIE WELL SAUCE"* the waiter insisted.

For some inexplicable reason, the entire staff ignored the brand name, referring to it by the instruction on the label 'SHAKE WELL'.

In Italy, whilst well liked, it is called WORSTA SAUCE!

THE MOTOR MECHANIC

Two off duty Central African Airways engineers, Mike and John were working together on Mike's wife Mary's car. They wore company overalls.

With the engine in pieces, they discovered that they required a replacement part. Mary was asked to take Mike's car and armed with the 'part number' go and buy a new one.

The two friends continued with other work. When Mary returned, she saw John going into the house, her husband lying on his back on a maintenance trolley under the car. His overalls were completely unbuttoned and wearing no underpants, they revealed his 'manhood'.

Mary tiptoed up to the car, she slipped her hand inside his trousers giving him a good jerk. There was a yell and a thump of head meeting the underside of the car. Mary took off at speed for the relative safety of the house anticipating being followed by her husband, instead she ran into his arms, as he exited the house!

The 'lucky' man, under the car, was a third engineer friend who had come over to help out.

 # ENTHUSIASM

Throughout one's career, one hears numerous seriously pertinent and penetrating 'one liners'. My favourite is

"THOSE *NOT FIRED* WITH ENTHUSIASM. WILL BE *FIRED* WITH ENTHUSIASM".

THE WORLD SOCCER CUP

QUESTION.
Why are Pakistan never in the World Soccer Cup?

ANSWER.
Because, every time they would be awarded a 'corner' they would open a Newsagent's Shop.

COMPLAINT to AEROFLOT

In British European Airways circa 1950, we were faced with a major ticketing problem because of a 'cock-up' by an Aeroflot Ticketing Agent.

My supervisor wrote to Moscow and complained.
The reply was not merely apologetic. We were led to believe, that the Agent responsible would be 'shot every morning for a week'.

We never wrote complaining to Aeroflot again!

BLACK MAMBA

In 1958, when based in Dar es Salaam with East African, we were spending the day with friends, the Walshes at Ukongwa, near Dar Airport.

After lunch, we were in the lounge enjoying coffee. Sambo, one of the Walshe's two cats, a favourite of Anne, came into the room and scurried behind the curtains.

In seconds, he appeared in front of Anne and jumped onto her lap presenting her with his prized possession a live BLACK MAMBA!

Anne, terrified of all snakes, performed a 'trick' that I am unlikely to see ever again.

Without disturbing the Parker Knoll armchair in which she was sitting, whilst facing the direction she was in, Anne climbed up and over the back rest, landing on her feet behind the chair! It happened so fast, that both Sambo and the Mamba just fell to the floor. A feat to behold indeed.

THE LIGHT PULL

On my first visit to Stockholm circa 1952, I was met by a colleague in B.E.A Stockholm Office.

He counselled, that if I dated a Swedish girl, I should not try to kiss her outside her front door. It is very much frowned upon. If she invites you in, then the sky's the limit!

Having arrived late afternoon, Lars and I were to have dinner together. I decided to have a bath and a good soak when I got to my hotel.

Darkness comes in very fast late winter and I tried to switch on the light via the pull switch hanging over the 'tub'.

Nothing happened, well not until the bathroom door burst open and an enormous blond with 'old fashioned head phone' hair buns stood there. I tried to explain that all I wanted was to switch on the light. It had no effect, she promptly got to work with a long bath brush soaping it and applying it to my back etc. I decided the only thing to do was lay back and enjoy it.

UNIONS

Few know and many of those who do know, choose not to remember, that Unions came about because of bloody awful management.

Personally I favour good management but clearly recognise that staff are 'forced' to form or join unions for their own protection. I had to do this as late as 1976!

I am justly proud that on most of the stations I have managed, my staff chose not to join a union, believing that my approach was always fair and sensible. Discussion and compromise always prevailed.

Sadly the pendulum swings from one extreme to the other. The unreasonable extremists of both employers *and* unions rarely appear to learn the essentials of moderation, compromise, respect and negotiation.

If a company makes healthy profits, shares them with those who have played a vital part in making them or if the company is going through a bad period, explaining why and what needs to be done it will more likely survive and grow. Honesty pays.

What astonishes me, is the greed of certain directors of very big companies. Their boards have the gall to state that early retirements and redundancies are essential to growth and prosperity, that wages cannot be increased, everything has to be kept within inflation levels. They then award themselves outrageous increases or diamond encrusted golden handshakes.

Outlays which would fund the continued employment of scores of staff forced on to the dole with inhuman worries of how they are going to pay mortgages and/or feed their families.

One airline Personnel Director accepted early retirement (full pension & privileges) *PLUS* a golden handshake of $900,000 tax free. This figure would have kept 52 staff costing $17,000 (Pay roll costs included) employed for a year.

There are far too many examples of such greed and it amazes many managers senior and junior, as to why the top people fail to recognise the anger such actions breed. Believe me, they are never forgotten.

MISSION IMPOSSIBLE

As one would appreciate, many are the times when information passed from Head Office to their 'men' overseas is highly confidential. Such was the case, when my friend, our International Currency Controller sent me a memo which read

"Denis, the contents of this memo are so highly confidential that you must destroy it before reading it!"

I replied by telex.

"Have carried out the instructions in your memo xyz very carefully. Kindly forward another copy, as I have not the slightest idea what it is about or what I am expected to do next!"

 # THE HAYCART

A Flight Engineer who rather fancied himself as a Rally car Driver went on vacation to Ireland with his girl friend. He hired a high performance car and to make their driving more realistic, he set strict journey times, awarding himself penalty points at the end of each day.

One afternoon, running late along a sleepy country lane, he found himself following a huge haycart drawn by two drays.

Try as he may, he could not pass the haycart.
After 40 odd minutes of frustration, the haycart pulled well over to the left of the road.

Seeing his opportunity to overtake, our man dropped down into second gear and stood on the gas. Just as he was coming alongside the haycart, it pulled sharply to to the right. The Flight Engineer smashed into it 'amidships'

Furious, the Flight Engineer jumped out of his car, demanding of the farmer "Just what the hell do you think you were doing swerving to the left and then to the right without any warning?"

"What am I, doing? Sure don't I turn into this field every Thursday afternoon at half past three. Tis I who should be asking you what the hell are you doing" was the illogical response.

NEVER OUTSIDE his VILLAGE

Running the Arrival/Interline desk at Waterloo Air Terminal circa 1954, I received a call from Heathrow, advising that 'on coach registration number xxx, there was a very naive Irishman. Please meet and assist pointing him in the direction of Waterloo Railway Station", which was directly across the street from us.

I arranged for the passenger to be met and brought to me. I directed him through the Departures section telling him to exit left. On exiting, he would see the station directly in front of him. The passenger confirmed that he clearly understood.

About 20 minutes later, the Departures Supervisor a friend, invited me to join him for a Capuchino in 10 minutes. We were going to 'La Ronde', an Italian cafe just around the far corner of the railway station.

My friend and I met at the entrance to our terminal and walked towards the Zebra crossing. There on the curb was the Irishman, his baggage at his feet. Not thinking that it was 30 odd minutes since he left me, I asked if he was OK or if he needed any assistance. The poor man was 'glued' to the floor unable to cross the road he said that he had never seen so much traffic in his life. So much traffic!, it was 1630 Saturday afternoon, only the hours of 1900-0600 and all day Sundays were quieter. Sadly, he had never in his life been outside his remote village in Ireland. Rush hour there, was three cars an hour!

We assisted him cross the road, buy his ticket and seated him in the nearest compartment to the Guard's van. I then telephoned his sister, advising her exactly where he was seated, entreating her to be certain to meet him at Basingstoke.

PERCY & BORIS

Many airline men tell great stories and the best I heard was told by my friend and former colleague in British Caledonian Airways Advertising.

When on a big promotion in Caracas Venezuela, he related this one.

'Once upon a time, in a remote kingdom of Eastern Europe, there lived a king who was stony broke.

Boris the Bold the Bulgarian Baron, a filthy rich ugly man, knew well of the king's plight. He also knew, that the king had the most gorgeous daughter of 19 years. Boris the Bold, the Bulgarian Baron had tried unsuccessfully on numerous occasions to woo the lass.

He decided that the only way to succeed, was to get to her through her father. He made an appointment to see the king.

"Your Majesty, I, Boris the bold, the Bulgarian Baron, am in love with your daughter but she will have nothing to do with me. I am clearly aware of your financial plight and am willing to strike a deal. If you persuade your daughter to marry me, I will deposit in both your personal and state treasuries, enough money to ensure the comforts you and your people deserve to enjoy".

Delighted, the king agreed and sent for his daughter living in sin, deep in the forest with Percy the Pauper the Poor Persian Prince.

When she arrived, the king explained how she could help, not only her parents, but also her country by leaving Percy the Pauper the Poor Persian Prince, and marrying Boris the Bold, the Bulgarian Baron.

"But father, I love Percy the Pauper the Poor Persian Prince and loath Boris the Bold, the Bulgarian Baron" cried the lovely princess.

"I know, I know but you do not seem to appreciate the importance of the sacrifice I am asking you to make. Please accept the offer of Boris the Bold the Bulgarian Baron and the luxurious life he can provide *all* of us, instead of that impoverished awful existence with Percy the Pauper, the Poor Persian Prince" argued the king.

"It is no use father" the sobbing girl cried.

Frustrated, the king drew himself up to his full 5' 4" demanding an explanation of what was so important.

"Well father it is very simple. I prefer to have my pussy, pecked and pricked by the perfectly pointed penis of Percy the Pauper the Poor Persian Prince, than to have my buttocks bashed and banged by the bloody great balls, of Boris the Bold, the Bulgarian Baron".

A former colleague always had great difficulty relating this when sober. However, when he was well and truly 'oiled', he was word perfect. Sadly he was rarely able to appreciate the compliments of his admirers because he would 'go out like a light'.

A true tongue twister.

'WAIT & SEE'

The Agency Investigation Board (renamed Agency Investigation Panel), is the regulatory board governing I.A.T.A members and their Agents (Travel Agents) performance and behaviour. The Chairman and Secretariat were normally provided by the national carrier. Any member with a complaint against another member or Travel Agent has it investigated here. The Board is an arm of I.A.T.A regional office.The deliberations therein are supposed to be highly confidential, sadly they are not.

Alitalia Central Africa, often the subject of jealous accusations, advised the Secretariat, that they had a complaint against the national carrier Central African Airways. Confident that he knew what Alitalia were concerned about, C.A.A's rather forceful Chief Executive decided that he would attend the next board meeting and explain his carrier's position. Of course, the Secretariat had no option but to accede to his desire.

Kevin Nolan, Alitalia's Regional Sales Manager, who was to present their case, was described by the Chief Executive "As a very nice person, known for his rather excitable approach to such things". This was absolute rubbish, Nolan was the complete opposite. Softly spoken, he was a well educated, typical mild mannered gentleman of the Emerald Isle.

The C.Ex went on to say that he was well aware of Alitalia's gripe. "He would personally explain and clear the confusion. There would be no need for lengthy discussion" He went to great lengths explaining why C.A.A had taken certain questionable action, on a given activity.

Kevin sat quietly allowing the C.Ex tell, his story in full. At the finish, Kevin thanked the C.Ex for his frank and informative admissions over his Company's misdemeanour, however, this was NOT what Alitalia wished to complain about!

It was a salutary lesson in the need to listen before barging in with an inappropriate explanation.

THE LEBANESE

There are thousands of Lebanese throughout West Africa, sadly a great number have a much to answer for concerning their activities. Of course there have been a few who's contribution has been honest and beneficial and one must never forget, that many indigenous have been willing and excellent students of the questionable practices.

A prominent Sierra Leonean friend, who like so many of his countrymen, had no time for their 'guests', asked me to describe the Lebanese.

I said that they are Asians of Arabic descent, who inhabit a land on the Eastern shore of the Mediterranean".

"No, no not at all, it is much simpler than that" said my friend. They are men, who can enter a revolving door after you and exit it ahead of you!"

 ## TRUCK DRIVER

A high percentage of a European carriers' flight deck crew training, took place in the relatively quiet air space over Shannon in Eire. As an economy measure, they retained a couple of spare engines at Shannon.

On his first visit to Ireland, one truck driver delivering an engine, encountered a major delay on the main road. He decided to try the back roads to save time. He diligently studied his maps for a clear alternative routing.

Unfortunately, at one fork junction, some idiot had erected a sign incorrectly. Believing that his new route would be safe for his oversized vehicle, he proceeded. En route he tried to pass under a bridge which had no height restriction warning. As the truck passed under, or rather tried to pass, it became firmly wedged. Very angry, the driver climbed out of his cab. While contemplating his problem, a member of the Garda (Irish State Police Force) from a nearby village appeared on the bridge.

He parked his bicycle against the wall on which he leaned, calling out,

"Are ya stuck?" The driver, in no mood for humour replied,

"Oh no, I was *delivering* this bridge and I got lost!"

"IS YOUR TICKET 100% FREE?"

When based in Nairobi, I was asked to return to Lusaka Zambia and help my company sort out a problem developing a new marketing strategy.

Armed with a free Duty Travel ticket with Up Grade to First Class, I was standing by at Embarkasi Airport. I reported to 'Check In' and took up station on the crush bars about 7 metres in front of them. After sitting there about 35 mins, a gentleman came up and asked "Is your name Denis Long?" I replied "Who is asking?

After repeating his question, he added "I am a Queen's Messenger (British Diplomatic Courier), if you are Denis Long, British and your ticket is 100% FREE, you may, if you are prepared to suffer a few bags around your feet, travel alongside me". Often the 'dip' bags contained documents of such highly confidential nature, they *HAD* to travel in sight of the courier. Frequently this necessitated the purchase of a second seat. The seat next to the courier was always kept vacant by the airline. If they did not cooperate, it would be the end of their participation in this most lucrative of business.

The courier went on "I am not prepared to allow this lot earn a single penny more at our expense. Since my 'firm' has paid for two seats, providing that your ticket is 100% free, you are welcome to join me"

SECOND HIGHEST

The town roads in Sierra Leone were, for many years in the eighties, in a sorry state. Government Ministers, senior civil servants and top businessmen bought Mercedes Benz cars to help cope with them!

At the beach, I was introduced to two visiting M.Benz Engineering Inspectors, quality checking their agent. I asked them "Is it true, that Sierra Leone is the second highest 'per capita' purchasers of their fine cars?" "No it is not" they said in unison, with a wry smile.

"Ah then, they are possibly third, fourth or may be fifth highest" I said with a sigh of relief. How could a country, categorised in the 10 poorest on earth, even be fifth? "They are number ONE" said the engineers. "Per Capita, they are our best customers world-wide!"

 # THE SISAL BARON

In the late forties, early fifties in Kenya, an elite band of farmers grew sisal, used in rope and mat making and became very rich. They became known as 'The Sisal Barons'. One an Englishman, used my office for all his travel requirements. His plan for his next overseas travel, was to fly to London, pick up a Rolls Royce, tour England and Europe, hand over the car in Italy and fly Rome Nairobi.

While in Austria, the car broke down close to a delightful little village. The 'farmer' and his wife, walked to the only hotel and telephoned the U.K. Rolls Royce asked if the hotel was satisfactory, if not, please take a taxi to one more fitting their status.

Rolls would reimburse all expenses. Further Rolls would contact their nearest representative who would examine the car and report back. They in turn would brief the 'farmer'. The couple were perfectly happy to remain where they were.

By 1600 hours, a gentleman informed them, that he had advised U.K of his findings, Rolls were flying out four engineers and spares A.S.A.P. Next morning, the arrival of the chartered DC3 at the little used airport was the talk of the entire village. The Chief Engineer reported his presence adding that repairs would take six to seven hours. In fact, the car was ready by 1700 but the couple decided to stay the extra night. The RR Senior Engineer paid the hotel bill, apologised for the inconvenience, wishing their clients a trouble free continuation of their journey. The rest of the journey, as was the car's service in East Africa, was trouble free.

On their return to Kenya, the 'farmer' wrote a letter of appreciation to Rolls, not only of their excellent P.R approach but for their prompt and efficient reaction .

Rolls reply read 'We thank you for your appreciation of our overall service, which we will as always, strive to maintain. However, we can find no record of any breakdown in continental Europe.'

A VERY FAMILIAR VOICE

One lunch in a very crowded 'Pub', I was at the counter picking up my order. Having six glasses balanced on my tray, I turned onto my blind side and bumped into a large man with a very familiar voice. Having apologised, he said 'No problem boyo'

"Good God, 'Taffy Jones" , (one of my favourite B.C.A.L engineers) says I. "Less of a problem than my recent experience" he said. I asked for an explanation.

"In a saloon bar in a small Texas town last month, I did exactly as you did. With 6 glasses firmly in two hands, I turned and bumped into a man, much bigger than myself, I apologised as you have done". "I have killed men for less than that" a very familiar voice said, a cold shiver went right through me. It was John Wayne!"

 # RED INDIAN CHIEF

An Englishman was sipping his 'G & T' in a saloon in a quiet town of Arizona, when a Red Indian Chief , in full regalia strode in and up to the bar. He wore a '45', carried a plastic bag full of horse manure with a cat on his shoulder. "BEER", the Chief said,

The Englishman was fascinated. The Chief swallowed the pint in one swig, threw the plastic bag into the air and from the hip shot a number of holes in it.

The petrified cat took off at great speed under the swing doors with the Chief in hot pursuit. The Englishman's fascination turned to incredulity because no one, not even the bartender, turned a hair.

The Englishman asked the bartender "What is going on?"
Bartender, "I have no idea, every Monday, Wednesday and Friday evening this happens. On Saturday evenings, he comes in and pays a very fair price for cleaning up the mess".

Wednesday evening, the Englishman was anxiously awaiting the arrival of the Chief in the saloon. As the Chief came in, the Englishman approached him "May I ask why you go through this routine three times every week?"

"Me train to become airline salesman" said the Chief.

"You are what?", the astonished visitor queried.

"Ya, I told to 'Drink piss, shoot shit 'n chase pussy all day".

THINK ABOUT IT!

Some cultures feel that they must always come out on top, Frequently, this approach comes from a lower level of society having a need to assert their 'power'. To illustrate:

IN A WEST AFRICAN COUNTRY.

A missionary I know very well, was highly respected amongst the indiginous community. Driving into the city, he stopped at the Traffic Lights close to the National Stadium. Awaiting the red to change to green, he was shocked to feel another car run into the back of him. Fortunately, the damage was minimal, whatever the missionary got out of his car to collect the usual insurance details. A policeman, appeared from nowhere and before the 'man of God' uttered a word, the policeman said

"You know padre, it is forbidden for cars to reverse at Traffic Lights!"

Another tale was that of the wife of the General Manager of a major petroleum company. One morning, she telephoned her husband with "That's it, I have had all I can take of this place. Driving into town this morning, I stopped at the Traffic Lights at the XYZ junction. A policeman walked over and informed me that I had crossed the white line. Protesting, I pointed out that there was none. "Ah madam, you see, you have passed over the point where the white line <u>should</u> have been painted!"

THE MISCOUNT

The Passenger services Agent (PSA) came to me at the Departure Gate, "We are one down, in spite of having the correct number of boarding passes!, I have double checked".

"Why do you think you are one down, if your boarding passes are correct? check again!" We expected 25 passengers, standing at the coach entrance, I counted only 24 heads. However, when I counted my boarding passes I had 25. She did another head count-still minus one.

I climbed on board the coach which was due to take the passengers out to their aircraft. As I walked to the front of the coach, I said "Ladies & Gentlemen, we have collected 25 boarding passes and yet there are only 24 passengers on board. Does anyone know of a travelling companion who may have disembarked?" No response. At the front of the coach, I turned, as I started to count, a shawl slipped off a young mother's shoulder, she was breast feeding her infant.

The missing head! Today, most carriers issue 'Infant & Child' boarding passes. These immediately alert staff. When we do get a 'One Down' situation, we are faced with a major problem. It could be a classical way of getting a terrorist device on board an aircraft and not travelling. e.g. A passenger checks in with his baggage and then disappears. When it happens, we off-load all the passenger baggage, we then disembark all the passengers who are required to personally identify their bag(s), these and only these are reloaded. On a full B747, this exercise can take up to three hours!

AFRICAN TIME KEEPING

Is a problem which I believe most new expatriates in Africa take time to come to terms with. Having spent 32 years in East, Central and West Africa. West Africa is clearly the worst.

In West Africa, we scheduled dinner parties to start at 2000 for 2030 hours.

Most guests would turn up in good time, sadly our African guests frequently the principal guest(s) were invariably late or did not pitch up at all.

Initially, we would wait until close to ruining the meal, out of deference to them. Eventually, we learned to start at the stated time. Two cases demonstrate why.

The first concerned an invitation to the Minister of Transport, the minster with whom I had considerable contact and our principal guest. Having waited until we could wait no longer we started without them. They never showed up.

Next morning, genuinely concerned, I called the Minister's Office to enquire re his well being. "Are you or your wife unwell?" I enquired.

"No we are both very fit" the Minister confirmed.

"Then what happened to you last evening, you acknowledged my invitation?"

"Oh, we were not hungry!" he replied.

The second incident concerned another Minister and his wife. They too did not turn up. This time I did not telephone him, knowing that we were to attend the same meeting with the president at State House next day. Before I said anything, he volunteered his explanation. "Sorry we did not get to your dinner party, we were on our way". I was fascinated. "As we passed the Roxy Cinema, my wife noticed that Kramer vs Kramer was showing. I have been wanting to see that for months, we are not going to miss it this time, she said!

An American Ambassador to one West African state, organised a dinner party for 24 including his British counterpart and his wife. There were 20 nationals guests. At start time, only the Brit, the American and their wives were in attendance. In the event, NO OTHER guests made it. The four ate alone!

STATE HOUSE GIG

At a West African station I ran, I was always first in each morning, my secretary was normally close behind me. On the morning in question, my secretary was delayed. I decided to type a note to my expatriate Sales Manager in my secretary's name. I prayed that she would get in before him. She made it with seconds to spare. The note read:

"State House, secretary to the Cabinet called. You are required to report there (Secretary's Office) at 1130 today and explain your actions". The note was placed in the middle of the S.M's desk. When he came in, he studied the note for a few minutes and then asked my secretary "If anything else was said?" "No, not another word" she advised. He knocked on my door. "Have you seen this Denis?" he asked "I have, what the hell have you been up to?" I queried. "Nothing, nothing" he protested. I went in again "Have you been chasing a Government Minister's wife, or that of a senior Civil Servant?"

"No, no" he assured me. "You had better think very hard, off you go" said I. He returned to his desk and took out all of his files, each of which he scoured in the hope of finding a clue. To help him at State House, I offered him my car and driver who knew it well. My driver would park the car and await the S. M's exit.

My driver had to deliver a quantity of promotional material to a club for a function that evening. When at the club, our brand new Peugeot 505 would not start. Having tried all he knew, my driver called in on the company radio. We had great difficulty in getting the Peugeot agent's mechanic up to the club. Added to that, a medical case had landed on my desk. Being 100% absorbed in it, I forgot both the Sales Manager and my driver.

For once in her laid back life, the Airport Manager's secretary used her initiative and tried to arrange for the A.P.M's driver to take over from mine on the State House duty. This almost caused a catastrophe. my driver had been briefed that we were teasing the S.M and on how he was to participate. Fortunately, my driver returned in the nick of time and collected the S.M.

He drove to state House grounds with the S.M still totally confused as to what he had to 'explain'. As he was about to drop the S. M, he accelerated away saying "April fool Sah" The S.M took the joke very well.

TB or VD

A Passenger Services Duty Officer at Gatwick, was determined to make love to a dizzy blond Passenger Services Agent later that day.

In his 'chat up' during their coffee break, she said that she had been feeling off colour and that she saw the company doctor the previous morning.

"Hope it is nothing serious" our beau said.

"Well I'm not sure, I have a terrible memory and cannot recall if the doctor said I had a slight touch of TB or VD!"

Our 'hero', frustrated and concerned, decided to call the doctor and try to establish what was wrong with the girl. "Do you recall seeing a dizzy attractive blond yesterday, I am concerned about her, she cannot recall if you said she had a slight touch of TB or VD. You see we are having a night out tonight and she has hinted at my stopping over".

"Well er, yes I did see an attractive blond, in fact I saw two but cannot recall which was which" the doctor nervously advised.

"What the hell am I to do? the frustrated Duty Officer pleaded.

"Oh that's very easy. When you get to her place, find some excuse to chase her for a few minutes, if she coughs, you can screw like hell" the doctor counselled.

DAY OLD CHICKS

An Irish Steward working for a British Airline, was laid off due to the recession which lasted a long time. Signing on at the *JOB CENTRE* every Monday over the past six months, he was delighted to hear that he was selected to participate in a new project.

Allocated 5,000 Day old Chicks, a piece of land, he lease purchased a small van . He received instructions to ensure that each chick was allocated at least 6" space, he left full of enthusiasm.

Two days later, he was back at the Job Centre. "They are all dead sir, all dead" he reported.

Very well liked, the sympathetic project organiser provided another 2,500 chicks. Next day, 'Paddy' was back again. "They are all dead sir, all dead" he pathetically reported.

"What do you think is the problem?" the organiser queried.

"Well sir, I am not exactly certain. I not sure if I am planting them too deep or too far apart!"

RACE RELATIONS

A husband and wife who flew for the same airline, found themselves operating a service on which there was a black steward who was tremendously popular with all his colleagues.

As a gesture towards improving race relations, they invited him to their forthcoming family Sunday picnic beside a lovely river.

After a most convivial and sumptuous lunch, they decided to work off the calories with a game of throwing a basket ball.

The teenage daughter and their guest were positioned close to the bank of the river. When the ball was thrown by the mother to her daughter, it passed clear over her head and into the water. The gallant guest dived straight into the river, swam, like a champion retrieved the ball firing it from the river back into play.

As he climbed out of the water, the silly daughter threw the ball to him, so high that the steward had to leap high into the air to stop it going back into the water. As he stretched, his shorts slid right down to his ankles, revealing a man well above ample proportions.

The family all stood with their eyes wide open and mouths gaping.

Clearly very very embarrassed, the 'guest' excused himself with "Does yours not shrink when it's cold and wet?"

WHAT COLOUR AM I?

A visitor to our Accra office from head office Gatwick needed to get to a meeting at the other end of the city.

My driver was off sick and I was tied to an equally important meeting in my office. Our guest asked if he could take my car. In town, he was stopped by an angry traffic police Officer controlling traffic.

"What colour am I?" demanded the 'cop'.
Thinking he could fall into some sort of trap, our visitor tried desperately to think of an alternative description for black.
He could not and said,

"Why black of course"

"I'm not talking about that" the irritated cop replied. Holding his right arm up straight and his left arm out horizontal to the ground, the cop said When I'm like this, I'm red. With his right arm beckoning towards my friend and his left arm at his side, he said Now I'm green and don't you forget it next time!"

UNCLE CHARLIE

An Air Canada friend told me of an Royal Canadian Mounted Policeman pilot who was required to fly to a remote settlement, way up in the Arctic Circle. Being so far, it was arranged that he would night stop

At dinner, with his hosts, a neighbour called in and asked the pilot "If he would take uncle Charley down to Toronto".

"No problem, I understand that your house is close to the airport. I'll call in on my way and pick him up", said the affable 'Mountie' .

Next morning, the 'Mountie' pulled into the driveway and after enjoying a coffee, enquired if uncle Charley was ready. He was anxious to get underway. "Oh he has been ready for some time, he is out in the back shed could you give us a hand with him?

Surprised, but always willing to help, the pilot accompanied the husband and wife to the shed. There he saw uncle Charley frozen solid. He had died whilst working in the shed some months earlier and was frozen stiff when they found him. As the old man had always expressed a desire to be buried in his place of birth, they simply waited for an aircraft to fly him down there.

 # 'SIGNS'

Two signs, both in an African country one at a northern Regional airport the other at the Capital City airport, were the sources of a few smiles in the 70's.
The northern sign read

"XYZ AIRWAYS FLIES
BACKWARDS *and* FORWARDS
TO LONDON"

At the capital city airport the sign read

**"XYZ AIRWAYS FLIES DAILY to LONDON,
except TUESDAYS, THURSDAYS,
FRIDAYS & SUNDAYS"**

MAGIC

With unfortunate regularity, a number of *certified* consignments of gold, handed in at Rome for London, were each found to contain an equivalent weight of lead, when opened at the consignee's office. Packing appeared untouched.

Security was stepped up with checks at packing, when handed in, at transfer from the Precious Cargo cage to the aircraft, from the aircraft to U.K Customs, from Custom to the Precious Cargo Cage and from here to the consignee strong room. Yet still, the switch was being made.

Security decided, that the switch *had* to be being made in the Precious Cargo area warehouse. With maximum secrecy, a security officer was placed in a large box, armed with a flask of coffee and a supply of 'sarnies'.

A very clever spy-hole was positioned to facilitate surveillance of the 'troublesome' consignment.

The gold arrived and with tight security, it was locked in the huge cage.
All staff withdrew.

An hour or so later, a very cleverly disguised trap door opened in the floor of the cage. An exceptionally careful 'artist' opened the consignment switched contents and expertly re sealed the package with seals. There was, as previously no trace of interference. As the trap door closed, the surveillance officer radioed his observations. The 'net' was drawn very tightly around the building and a very shaken thief surrendered.

INTERPRETERS

The vast majority of airlines, have amongst their Passenger Handling Staff, linguists of varying degrees of competence. At times, we in British European

Airways circa 1950, could provide between 25 and 30 different language on a shift. The total number spoken by all staff in their London Air Terminal was 57. One day, a passenger walked up to Arrivals Desk and spoke in a language, that the Anglo-Greek Passenger Services Agent could not understand. Thinking it resembled a Latin language, she called Roy Calderon (whose cartoons are in this book), a multi-lingual speaker of exceptional ability.

At the Arrivals Desk, Roy began 'Bon giorno Snr' no response. 'Bounos dias Snr', Bon jour Mes: nothing worked, it was hopeless.

Just as Roy was about to try one of his numerous other languages, two people came into the Arrivals Hall speaking in loud pronounced East London accents. Our 'foreigner' leapt to his feet saying, in the most pronounced Cockney accent, "Oi guv, can you elp mi git som info outa this bleedin lot?"

AEROSOLS

One of the most effective of all 'aerosols I ever bought, was one I picked up in Florida.

Whenever I was to see a person known for his 'line shooting' I would position the can on my desk in a prominent position. If the name on the can did not have the desired effect, I would lift it and spray the air (the contents was a simple air freshener).
The label read "BULLSHIT REPELLENT".

It *never failed to work* and was worth every cent I paid for it.

FUNNIES

Over the years I have heard a number, here are a few which I trust you will enjoy.

BOREN'S LAW of BUREAUCRACY.
   a) When in doubt, mumble.
   b) When in trouble, delegate.
   c) When in charge, ponder

BEAURQART's LAW
   'When you're up to your nose, keep your mouth shut.

BOYLE's LAW.

"If not controlled, work will flow to the competent person until they submerge".

DONAHUE'S LAW.

"What is worth doing, is worth doing for money"

MURPHY's LAWS.

"It is impossible to make anything fool proof, because fools are so ingenious".and "If anything can go wrong, it will go wrong" and "To err is human, but to really foul things up, requires a computer!

ABBOTT's admonitions.

a) If you have to ask, you're not entitled to know".

b) If you don't like the answer, you should not have asked the question.

LIMERICK

'There was a young woman from Wantage,
of whom the Town Clerk took advantage.
Said the Borough surveyor:
"You surely must pay her,
for you've completed altered her frontage".

MAN IN A PUB.

"Funny how my wife can spot blonde hairs but not miss the garage doors"

QUEENS' REGULATIONS

Guests in a Cairo hotel during 1943, heard screams and shouts. They saw a damsel in her negligé being pursued by a nude man, wearing only an army officer's cap. He was apprehended and found to be a Major of the British army. He was. promptly court martialled.

His defence lawyer, a brother officer, won him a reprieve by virtue of the following paragraph in the Queen's Regulations.

"It is not compulsory for an officer to wear uniform at all times, as long as he is suitably garbed for the sport in which he is engaged!"

PISSED.

A young lady trying to impress at her first cocktail party:
"I have only had tee Martoonies. I'm not as drink as thinkle pople I am, but I fool so feelish and the drunker I sit, the longer I get"!

AN OLD CASTILIAN SAYING.

"An after dinner speech, is like the horns of a bull. It has a point here and a point there, and an awful lot of bull in between".

THE DUKE AT DINNER.

An elderly Duke was a guest at a dinner party. At his club, the next day, he was asked by a friend how he enjoyed his evening. The Duke replied with a sigh. 'Well, if the melon had been as cold as the soup, the soup had been as warm as the claret, the claret had been as old as the chicken, the chicken had been as young as the waitress, and the waitress had been as willing as the Duchess. I could have had a damn good evening!

THE SWIMMING POOL.

A headmaster of a 'prep' school in the 1930s was much concerned at the deteriorating quality of the water in the school swimming pool.

He sent off a sample to the local analyst. In due course, a detailed report was provided. It ended with the following. "This horse is past work and should be humanely destroyed as soon as possible!"

SPOONERISM and BLOOPERS.

An English vicar with a sense of humour, when performing a marriage ceremony said "you are now joyfully loined" instead of "you are now lawfully joined!"

Two innocent bloopers by teachers.

a) A male teacher was passing a classroom from which emanated a great deal of noise including a strange (funny) most irritating sucking sound. The teacher opened the door and in a firm authoritative voice said, "Stop that sunny f*****g noise'!

b) In a co-educational school with a large playground, the Head Mistress would frequently order boys to 'Play with your balls at the far end of the playground".

Another spoonerism.

What is the difference between Eleanor Roosevelt and the Panama Canal?" The canal is a busy ditch!

GRAFFITI.
   Seen:
On the London Underground
"God loves Black & White" *Graffito* "But He prefers Johnnie Walker"

Outside a London church.
"Jesus saves" *Graffito* "But only at the Halifax".

In the Meteorology office
"Wet paint" *Graffito* "Drier later".

Seen on the London UNDERGROUND
'I HATE GRAFFITI, IN FACT, I DISLIKE ALL ITALIAN FOOD'

DISCUSSION BETWEEN TWO EXPATRIATES OVERHEARD IN A BAR IN SINGAPORE.

Q/ When were you last in the U.K?
A/ On, some years ago. At the time they made homosexuality legal.
Q/ When do you plan your next visit?
A/ Never, I'm afraid that they might make it compulsory!

@@@@@@@@@@@@@@@@@@@@@@@@@@@@

"Y'know, being married ruins your sense of humour".

"Marriage is *not* a single word, it is a bloody life sentence".

After a night of passionate love, a married couple having marital problems were at breakfast. He with a smarmy grin was shocked to hear his wife say "Marriage is a finely tuned machine, which one *screw* will not fix!"

@@@@@@@@@@@@@@@@@@@@@@@@@@@@

An Irishman suspected his wife of infidelity and began to follow her movements. Coming home from work early one afternoon, he burst into the bedroom catching his wife in bed with her lover. In a rage, he put his revolver to his own head. His wife started to scream with laughter. "Don't laugh, you are next!" he shouted.

@@@@@@@@@@@@@@@@@@@@@@@@@@@@

METRIC.

Paddy went into his local Greengrocers and asked for "Six pounds of potatoes". The shopowner advised him "Paddy they are no longer called that, they are kilos".

"OK. let me have six pounds of kilos then" said Paddy!

@@@@@@@@@@@@@@@@@@@@@@@@@@@@

How can you tell when there is an Irishman at the cockfight?
He enters the duck.
How do you tell which is the Pole?
He bets on the duck!
How can you tell which is the Italian?
The duck wins and he collects!

@@@@@@@@@@@@@@@@@@@@@@@@@@@@

Did you hear of the Pole who read that 90% of all accidents happen in the home? He moved!

Two Poles walked into a Post office, the first thing that caught their eye, was a WANTED poster which listed various crimes.

There was a photograph of an ethnic minority member WANTED for Rape. One Pole said to the other,
"You know, those guys always get the best jobs!"

@@@@@@@@@@@@@@@@@@@@@@@@@@@@

Joe Kwaaski, a Polish emigrant in the U.S.A was filled with excitement at the promise his new home held.

Getting into a taxi at the airport, he says to the driver "Tak mi to the YIMCA Hotel". Confused, the cabby goes to another cabby seeking his help. His friend says "Bet he's Polish, if he is, he wants the Y.M.C.A Hostel. They all go there". Joe is surprised when the cabby asks "Are you Polish?" It must be my accent he thinks. He resolves to study until he has no accent.

After months of study, Joe decides to check out his mastery of pronunciation. He goes to the corner store and in a perfect English accent orders, a pint of milk, a dozen eggs, a loaf of bread, a quarter of a pound of cheese.

"Are you Polish or something?" the shop assistant asks.

"Polish but how did you know. Did I not pronounce everything well?" replied Joe.

"You said everything just fine, but this is a hardware store!"

@@@@@@@@@@@@@@@@@@@@@@@@@@@@

Did you hear of the Polish designed parachute? It opens on impact!

@@@@@@@@@@@@@@@@@@@@@@@@@@@@

'Define 'Tragic Waste'.
It is observing a coach load of lawyers plunge over a 2,000' cliff with three empty seats.

@@@@@@@@@@@@@@@@@@@@@@@@@@@@

A hundred dollars prize was on offer at the circus, to the person who could make the elephant nod his head up and down. Dozens tried but failed.

Finally a little old man walked over to the elephant and grabbed it by the balls.The elephant trumpeted, throwing its' head up and down. The old man collected.

Next year, the circus was back again with a *similar* contest. This time they qualified the rules with a sign, "The elephant must not be touched, aft of the ears and the animal must also shake his head from side to side".
The same old man pitched, number 1209 to try. He walked over to the elephant and whispered "Remember me?" The elephant shook his head up & down.
The old man then whispered "Want me to do to you what I did last year?" The elephant fiercely shook his head from side to side!

@@@@@@@@@@@@@@@@@@@@@@@@@@@@

THE TROUBLES.
Two farm labourers working in Ireland found three hand grenades in a field. They agreed to take them to the village Police Station. As they walked down the country lane, Pat said to Mike "What if one of these dam things goes off?" Mike replied with "Will you stop worrying Pat, if it happens, we just tell the Police we only found two!"

142

TROUBLE MAKERS

The Benidorm charter flight developed a problem just as the passengers assembled in the allotted Gate area at Gatwick.

Being mid summer, the main departure lounge was packed tight. There was no alternative but to hold the passengers at the Gate.

As time dragged on, the passengers became restless. A group of five young men and women decided to make a nuisance of themselves by systematically going to the Podium asking silly questions. They also mounted a campaign of 'winding up' the other passengers. Having spent all their Sterling at the bar, they started on their Duty Free purchases. Asked to desist, they became even more obnoxious.

The Passenger Services Agent in charge of the Gate spotted a Customs Officer walking past and beckoned to him.

After explaining how the group of passengers were behaving and they were well into their Duty Free purchases, the Customs Officer wandered over to them asking if he could examine their purchases, 'just to ensure that the seals were intact you understand'. "Oh dear, oh dear, what have we got here? You are of course aware of the law demanding that Duty Free purchases *must* not be opened until *after* your flight has taken off". The slob from whom the officer had taken a half empty bottle of liquor, became aggressive, As if he was not already in enough trouble, the Officer threw the book at him.

"Now lets see,
a) You are in violation of not simply breaking the seal on the Duty Free bag, but of opening a bottle of alcohol. You have in effect, opened all the contents.

b) Duty must now be paid on
    i)   The 2 litre Whiskey.
    ii)   The 1.5 litre Brandy.
    iii)   The 1 kilo box of liquor chocolates.
    iv)   The 500 King size cigarettes.

That comes to £25 please. I can accept cash and most major credit cards. More abuse from the slob was closed down by a short lecture on the Officer's powers and "Hold on, I am not finished"

c) You have to pay 25% of the total value as a fine. This adds another £19, giving us a total of £44 please.

Now somewhat subdued, the 'slob' in a cockney voice said "I ain't got no sterling or credit cards". The Officer finished with "I can accept Spanish Pesetas but if you are out of them also, then I'm afraid it has to be no pay, no go."

The other four had quietly deserted *their friend* and the general ambience of the Gate area became very calm!

 # GENESES

Shortly after my transfer to Sierra Leone, a domestic who was to stay with me (10 years) until I retired him at 76 on a pension, told me the Creole version of the First Book of The Old Testament. I believe it worthy of retelling.

"For de furst tim, no thing deh! An de Lawd, He done go work ard for make dis ting dey call um hhearth. Fur six day, de Lawd, He work an He done make all ting.

Everyting Ge put fur hhearth. Plenty beef, plenty cassava, plenty groudnut, plenty banana, plenty yam, plenty guinea corn, plenty mango, everyting. An fur de watta, He put plenty fis, in da hair, He put plenty kinda bird.
Afer six day, de Lawd, dun gò sleep.

An when He sleep, plenty palava start fur dis place call um eaven. Dis eaven, be place where we go live when we dun die, if we no bin so-so bad fur did earth. De angel dey live fur even an play de banjo an git plenty fine chop an plenty palm wine. De ead of dem angel, dey call um Gabriel.

When dis palava start fur eaven, dere be plenty humbug by de bad angel, dey call Lucifer. An Gabriel dun catch Lucifer an go flogg um. An palava dun stop one tim. De Lawd tell Gabriel, he be good man, too much an he go dash (give present), Gabriel one very fine trumpet. An Gabriel go git licence for play dis trumpet an hit de drum fur eaven.

Now Lucifer, he go fur ellfire where he be eadman now.
After de Lawd come go lookum, dis tim dey call earth an he savvy dat no man be fur seat. So de Lawd take small piece earth an He go breath an man be deh.

De Lawd, He say to Hadam, Hadam, an Hadam he say 'Yessah, an de Lawd say 'Hadam, you see dis garden dey call um paradise. Everyting fur dis garden be fur you , but dem mango tree dat be fur middle of garden, dat no be fur you. Da chop be 'whitman chop, it no be blackman chop. You no go chop um or you git plenty pain for belly, you savvy O?'

De Lawd, He don go back fur eaven to listen Gabriel play de trumpet an hit de drum.

Hadam, he go walka – walka fur garden where everting be fine too much. By an by, de Lawd He come back fur garden, He go lookum see Hadam.

De Lawd, He say 'Hadam, everting be all right, you like um?'. An Hadam, he say, 'Yessah Lawd, evertring no be bad, but', an de Lawd He say 'Wassamatter Hadam, you done git small trouble?'

Hadam he say 'No ah no git trouble Lawd, but I no git uman' An de Lawd He say 'Hah, hah'. De Lawd, He make Hadam go sleep for one place. He go take small bone foe Hadam's side, dey call um *wishbone*. He go breath, an uman deh. An de Lawd He go call dis uman Heava. De Lawd, He go fur wake Hadam an say

'Hadam, you see dis uman Heava?
An Hadam he say 'Yessah Lawd, ah see um, she be fine too much O'
An de Lawd go way fur up to eaven an Hadam an Heava go walka, walka for garden where dehy go play plenty.

One day, when Hadam go for catch Barracutta, Heava dun take small walk an he meet um shnake. De shnake he say 'Hello, mornin O Heava, eckabbo'. An An Heava she say 'Mushayo'. Shnake he say 'Wassamatter Heava, why fur you no chop dem fine mango from tree fur middle of garden?' Heava say 'That be fine whitman chop. Dat no be blackman chop. Hadam say we git too much trouble, plenty for belly, if we go chop um'.

An shnake he say 'Hadam, he black fool. Dat chop be good for blackman jiss like whitman. You chop um, you like um'. Heava, she done chop um un like too much. She den put dat mango for Hadam groundnut stew, den der be plenty trouble for paradise one time.

Hadam an Heava, dey done savvy dey be naked, dey no git cloth, so dey put um hat fur head. By an by, one man dey call um Noah come for garden. Noah he headman fur Elder Demster Boat (shipping line) an he don take Heava for sail on lagoon, dey go make plenty for Hadam.

Den de Lawd dun come back fur hearth. He go call Hadam, but Hadam he no be fur seat. He go fear de Lawd too much, an he go for bush one tim.

Again de Lawd call Hadam. An Hadam he say with small voice 'Yessah Lawd'. De Lawd say 'Wassamatter Hadam, why you go fur bush?' An Hadam say 'I no git cloth Lawd, so ah no want for you see me naked' De Lawd he vexed too much,

'Wat ting dis, you go tell me?' He say 'Hah, Hah, you dun go chop dem mango tree in de middle of de garden' An Hadam say 'Ah no chop um Lawd, dem uman you dun make fur me, she put um in groundnut stew'.

Den de Lawd he go make plenty palava, an He say 'Make fur pack you bag an go one tim' An de Lawd, he drive Hadam an Heava from paradise.

With apologise to Creole speakers for changes to make it more easy for others to understand and enjoy.

ASK YOUR FIRST OFFICER

A 747 was on 'Long Finals' into Harare airport Zimbabwe.

A light aircraft, totally without clearance, slipped into the approach pattern ahead of the Jumbo.
The Air Traffic Controller(A.T.C) requested the Big Jet to reduce speed while he desperately tried to clear the minnow.
However, the 747 kept gaining on it.
The A.T.C, again requested the 'Jumbo' to throttle back.
Angry, the 747 Captain asked the Controller:
"Do you have any idea just what the 'stall speed' of an aircraft of this size is?"
The young A.T.C, *innocently* replied:
"No, but if you care to ask your First Officer, he might well have an idea".

'CRATE CLASS'

The 'DIKO CASE', wherein a Nigerian living in U.K, accused by his National Government of massive wrong doing was kidnapped, drugged, loaded into a crate and booked on a Nigeria Airways freighter flight to Lagos, achieved nationwide press cover in the U.K after his release.

Someone 'snitched' on the operation and Diko was let loose in the Freight Shed at Stanstead Airport London by Security Staff.

Some wit in B.C.A.L, designed a poster depicting an economy class seat in a wooden box. It carried the caption:

'CRATE CLASS'
'THE NEW *NO FRILLS* ECONOMY CLASS SERVICE
TO
NIGERIA.

"MINE'S A ...."

One day a rather mean pilot walked into an English Country Pub. The landlord, after greeting him said, "What's yours?"

The pilot replied, "Many thanks, I'll have a double Glenlivet"
After downing the whiskey, the pilot bid the landlord farewell and started to leave. The Landlord said, "Excuse me, but you have not paid for your drink!" The pilot replied, "That is not only true, but since you offered me a drink, I have no intention of paying" He exited quickly.

The months passed and the pilot once again visited the same Pub. "I know you, I recall your refusing to pay for a drink you ordered" said the Landlord.

"Not me, I have NEVER failed to pay my debts" the pilot replied indignantly.

"It is quite amazing, I was certain it was you. You must have a double" said the Landlord.

"Thanks, please make it a Glenlivet" said the pilot.

 # TRAVEL AGENTS

Moses was the greatest Travel Agent of them all. For forty years, he kept his group constantly on the move and fed them on packed lunches provided by heaven.

The next greatest is 'Thos Cook', however, after around 150 years in operation, they still have not learned the secret of parting the Red Sea! They should talk to Universal Studios!

DEPRIVATION

My friend and neighbour Jerry Rycroft, took an escorted tour of the Western U.S.A. in the mid nineties.

Amongst a great crowd of fellow travellers, was one with a tremendous sense of humour. Across the back window of their coach, he strung a sign, it read:

'SPENDING THE KIDS INHERITANCE'.

It drew a great many smiles.

FREEDOM of SPEECH

I sincerely believe, that there is no salesman or woman alive, who at some time in their business lives, would dearly love to tell their retailers their actual thoughts, when the all too often 'stupid' or unreasonable type of question is heard.

When based in New Zealand, I attended a presentation by the Manager of Mount Cook Airlines on the introduction of their new service Auckland Queens Town, that beauty spot in the far south.

As with most airlines who introduce Creative Fares (Fares which encourage a potential passenger to consider a certain destination Vs that already chosen or convince some one dithering over a selected one. Such offers have to have a number of restrictions attached to them e.g.

(a) Minimum or maximum stay.
(b) Must spend Friday, Saturday & Sunday nights at destination.
(c) Must travel on flights departing between 2000 and 0800 hours etc, etc. Such fares are frequently used in the building of Inclusive Tour Packages

i.e. Air Fare + Hotel Accommodation + Sightseeing + Ground Transfers and/or Car Hire or a combination thereof.

At the end of the presentation, exclusively to Travel Agents and other airlines, a travel consultant from a major world travel organisation chain asked questions.

One was of the 'inane' category, it queried an obvious restriction.

Mount Cook's Manager snapped back with "Because we bloody well say so" Every airline man and woman attending, envied the courage and strength of his position.

While Mount Cook, were competing with the then National Airways Corporation, since merged with Air New Zealand, it was clear that he had had enough of such stupid questions.

'MYLES'

No matter how much we love our children, they are often capable of driving one 'up the wall'.

My son, in the early months of his twentieth year, was in one of those infuriating moods. He simply would no take NO for an answer and kept pushing his luck. "If you do not give it a rest, I will invoke a seldom used, but nevertheless legal prerogative. I will apply to the High Court for a change to your name".

He looked at me with a quizzical eyes. "You will do what?" he asked.

With as straight a face as I could maintain, I replied "before you were born, your mother and I ran through numerous names both male and female for the forthcoming infant. If you were a girl, we would christen her Claire Denise, if a boy, we would love to call him Myles, but for his sake decided on Mark. For his sake, not even the most selfish of parents should call their son MYLES LONG.

"You would not dare" Mark exploded.

"Try me, all you need do, is persist with your nonsense. There is nothing you can do about it until six months after your twenty first birthday" I said very firmly.

It worked a treat!

THE GLORY of CHRISTMAS

My wife and I attended the magnificent "Glory of Christmas" pageant in the Crystal Cathedral at Tustin California in December 1990.

In the scene where Mary on a donkey, tells Joseph that she is very tired and cannot face a two day journey on a donkey to Bethlehem for the census. A very young child immediately behind us innocently said to his mother, in a loud clear voice.

"Mommy, why does she not go by plane then?"

EAST AFRICAN CUSTOMS

In the days of the East African Community, Zanzibar was outside the control of East African Customs. If one visited Zanzibar, on returning to the mainland, one had to clear Customs. The 'Spice Island' was something of a Duty Free Zone and as always, passengers felt there was a challenge to 'beat' in paying duty.

One 'smart Alec in East African Airways, was for ever trying to think up ways. His most effective was to wrap a a packet of sanitary towels in attractive paper.

This was placed smack in the centre of his suitcase to be immediately visible to the examining officer. In Customs, he was asked by an Asian (Moslem) Officer. "Vat you have for declare?" "Absolutely nothing, please look for yourself".

The Officer opened the suitcase and on eyeing the 'gift' demanded to know of the contents. "I have told you nothing to declare, examine it if you wish" he was told.

With a wicked grin, the Officer tore off the wrapping and opened the box. On seeing the sanitary towels, the Officer became visibly embarrassed. He slammed down the lid of the suitcase, as he instructed our friend to go.

BA SHUTTLE CREW

The last 'Shuttle' flight Heathrow Glasgow landed at Abbotsinch airport, its crew hurried around to the 'Check In' desk to travel as planned back to Heathrow, as passengers. "Sorry fully booked. You guys will have to night-stop and return on the first flight tomorrow". the Duty Officer informed them.

All the protestations about commitments early next day in the South were to no avail. Suddenly the most junior member of the six 'man' crew, a steward asked each of his colleagues to immediately give him £10 each and not to argue. Very surprised, they did as instructed.

The steward then handed the Duty Officer the £60 saying. "I wish to purchase a ticket to London".

Under BA's own rules, if one passenger buys a ticket on the 'Shuttle' and the scheduled flight is full, BA has to produce an extra aircraft and crew and operate the service.

They all got home that night.

'KOSHER'

The British Caledonian Airlines Sales Team, were on a 'ROAR IN'. A concerted research and sales drive in western U.S.A. It was called such, because our corporate emblem was the Lion Rampant of Scotland.

At the end of each days' slogging around Travel Agents, Consolidators and Commercial Houses, the team would meet and de brief.

One Sales Manager, an Australian, reported that he had made contact with a Travel Agent run by a Mr O'Reilly. Mr O'Reilly had *control* of around US$500,000 of ethnic business per month. He promised us, provided we were as good as we claimed to be, a very high percentage because of our Gallic 'ethnic' connection.

Our co ordinator was our Marketing Director Ian Ritchie. Ian, both delighted and impressed, asked "Is Mr O'Reilly Kosher?"

"Oh no, he is Irish!!" our Aussie explained.

'FOREIGN AFFAIRS'

The 'Secretary of State for Foreign Affairs', is the supremo in charge of the 'FOREIGN an COMMONWEALTH OFFICE' in H.M Government.

During my 35 years in foreign service, I frequently heard it referred to as the 'COMMON and FOREIGNWEALTH OFFICE!'.

 # FALCONS

It is not uncommon, for wealthy Arabs to take their beloved Falcons overseas with them, when they go away.

Since most (wealthy Arabs) fly and their feathered birds are generally well behaved, the Arab buys an additional seat in First Class for his bird.

Some Mid East carriers have a specially designed perch which clamps across the arms of a First Class seat. It has a metal tray, which fits snugly over the actual seat of the First Class chair.

A Falcon was booked on a flight to London and the perch was fitted. When the cabin crew joined their aircraft, the Flight Service Supervisor noticed that the 'droppings tray' had no protective newspaper on it. He ordered a junior steward to do the necessary. The junior complied.

When the F.S. Supervisor checked this had been done, he was scandalised. The wretched junior had used an Arabic newspaper. The F.S. Supervisor roared for this to be changed immediately for a Hindi language publication. "We cannot have the falcon shitting on the words of our people, Hindi is far more appropriate!"

SUN BLOCK

Did you hear of the Aer Lingus First Officer who was about to sun bathe on a tropical beach?

He asked his captain "What strength sun block do you think I should use?" "Strength eight" came the fatherly advice.

"Oh be jabers, I only have strength four. Do you think if I apply two layers, it will do the job?"

"MIND your LANGUAGE"

Flying with an old friend who was very 'up front' about his fear of flying, we were well into 'take off speed', when the captain reversed thrust and braked hard to bring the Viscount of Central African Airways to a very slow roll at Lusaka in 1963.

The Public Address came to life with the Captain apologising for having to take such action. He explained, "Just as we approached 'lift off speed', there was a complete wind reversal. While 99% of the time, take off would be perfectly safe, Central African were not in the habit of risk taking, not even 1%. We will continue rolling to the other end of the runway and give it A TRY from there".

My friend, who's knuckles were white, he was gripping the back of the seat in front of him so hard, looked at me and said "Give it a *TRY*, a *TRY* what on earth does he mean, give it a try, is he not certain?" I reassured him, that it was a colloquialism, adding "He is hardly likely to take any chances after aborting with only a 1% risk of a problem".

After landing, I spoke to Captain Denis Christian, also a friend, who accepted my friends comment, while promising to be more circumspect about his phraseology in future.

BR****** NIGHT-STOP

When operating the 'short haul' sectors of B.C.A.L, our crews would be rostered totally varying periods of work.

A London Paris operation, could be just one way, or two round trips separated by a rest of up to three hours at Gatwick. Alternatively, the crew could operate to say Paris, night-stop and bring the first service Paris London over next morning. A mere two hours flying over two days. These operation became known by their type e.g. a double Paris or a night-stop Paris.

One evening, passing through the airport terminal, I met a confused marketing colleague. He said that he had just greeted one of our stewardesses about to reported for duty. The lass had possibly the strongest Scottish accent of all.

"Where are you off to?" my colleague enquired.
"A Brothels night-stop" she replied hurrying by.
My colleague was speechless. "Just what the hell is going on, what are we into?" he asked me.

"Don't be such an ass, it is a BRUSSELS repeat BRUSSELS night-stop" I reassured him.

SELECTING CABIN CREW

When the chairman of an Arab carrier travels on his airline, it is an unwritten requirement, that the First Class cabin be staffed by European Cabin Staff. He does not particularly care to have those of the Asian ethnic groups.

On a planned visit to London, reservations were made and Crew Rostering 'took necessary action'. Due to a last minute change in plans, the Chairman did not fly as booked.

When the chairman rebooked, not one of his preferred European girls was available. The chairman was not amused!

THE MAFIA

With more Italians living in some U.S. cities than in the biggest cities of Italy itself, the North American market is of high importance to Alitalia.

Two Alitalia Sales Reps from Italy called on their friend, an Alitalia Sales Manager in one of the subject United States cities.

In discussion, they learned that Alitalia's revenue earning from its' two principal 'Italian' Agents in that city, was not only below target, it was down on the previous year.

The next day, the two visitors hired special outfits and visited both the ethnic agents. In each agency, dressed in white suits, black shirts, white ties, black breast pocket hankies, heavy dark sun glasses wearing black and white brogues, asked to see the manager. "We speak in Italian, in case you do not speak Scilliano dialect".

"We are very unhappy with your support of Alitalia, who is doing so much to help the home country economy. This *MUST IMPROVE* to the target figure given you. Make absolutely certain you reach it by the end of the year. Capice?" Without another word, they got up and left. Each Agency Manager, terrified, nodded his clear understanding of the message.

From that day on, reservations requests from each showed marked improvements.

One Travel Consultant advised the Alitalia Reservations Agent "That they had had strict instructions to 'push' AZ as hard as possible" This the Agent reported to her Manager, who in turn reported to his Sales Manager.

The 'visitors' were very severely reprimanded and apologies were made to the Travel Agencies proprietors.

However the 'initiative' had the desired effect. It brought home Alitalia's 'problem' to its' normally most productive agents.

OVERWORKED SALES REP

Back in the sixties, in an 'offline' location (an area some flight hours from company services) a Sales Rep of Alitalia, in the United States, in spite of always exceeding his targets, never stopped complaining of his work load.

His Regional Manager was very impressed until the man concerned was suddenly taken very ill. Doctors forecast that he would be away from the office for six to eight weeks.

"We had better organise a relief" decided the Regional Manager but he had none to spare. The best solution it was thought, was for the National Sales Manager in New York to go down. He could renew his contact with the market in that area.

When the 'relief' arrived at the 'off line office', way up in a skyscraper, he found a long queue of clients awaiting attention. He immediately joined the one Reservations Agent in the office. Between them, they comfortably handled a constant stream of passengers throughout the day. Naturally, the National Sales Manager enquired of the 'normal days work load'. He was advised that it was always that heavy, after all, our city has one of the biggest Italian populations outside Italy.

The office was upgraded, extra staff were employed and the Sales Target was dramatically raised, to cope with the far greater potential than the Sales Rep' cared to admit to. The next year Sales Target was not so easily achieved!

MY AUNTIE

An airline captain was having a rather passionate affair with one of the company's unaccompanied minors escorts, known as AUNTIES.

The captain concerned, was at the simulator for one of his regular checks, the 'Training Captain' was at the simulator controls.

After 'take off', the Training Captain introduced a series of wickedly difficult problems, the Captain under 'check' was made to struggle very hard to fly his 'aircraft' safely. He sweated blood throughout his ordeal.

On completion of the exercise, the Training Captain simply quipped "That will teach you to F*** my Auntie!"

 # UNMINS* of SENIOR STAFF

I have always held the belief that the children of senior staff, under the age of 15 should not be allowed to avail themselves of their parents privilege of First Class travel when travelling alone. The only exception being that they should not be left behind when Economy and Business Classes are full. Even then, every effort should be made to up grade suitable revenue passengers and seat the youngster in Economy.

My son Mark when 12, was making one of his frequent visits to us in Freetown. Dropped off by the school taxi, he made his way to the flight 'Check In' where he found a terrific queue. He nipped down to the First Class 'Check In' asking the lady Agent if she would check him in for Economy. On seeing the Up Grade stamp on his ticket, she checked the booked load. Finding 6 seats available, she advised Mark of this and that she was checking him into First class right away. Mark responded, "Thank you mam, but please just check me into Economy, my father does not approve of young staff passengers travelling alone in First Class.

Surprised, the Agent read Mark's surname and asked if his father's name is

Denis. Mark confirmed it was and the Agent added "Oh I know him well, he will not mind". I heard later, that Mark replied "Mam, I am afraid you do not know him anywhere as well as I do. If I travel First and there are seats available in Economy or Business Class, he will skin me alive. Please just check me into Economy".

On another occasion, well after Mark had checked in, he was in the *Chieftain* First Class lounge. Knowing well the lassies who manned the facility he was always allowed to sit quietly watching T.V after he had changed from his school uniform into jeans and sports shirt. An hour or so later, the Duty Officer came in asking Mark for his boarding pass. We have sold your seat and I am upgrading you to Business Class. Mark changed back into his school uniform. Jeans on staff not being allowed.

Half an hour later still, the Duty Officer appeared again up grading Mark into First having sold his Business Class seat. At the departure Gate, Mark was once again called over by the airside Duty Officer. "Afraid we have sold your First Class seat young fellow but no worry, the captain knows you and has agreed to your travelling on the flight deck. Mark changed yet again. He said a silent prayer, that the captain was one of his 'friendly' commanders. He loved travelling on the Flight Deck but in daylight or with a chatty crew. He hated long overnight flights with 'silent' crews. It is a very rare crew, who say almost nothing during daylight flights.

*UNMINS Airline jargon **Un**accompanied **Min**ors".

THE RIFT VALLEY

In the early sixties, Alitalia wanted to publish an aid to their offices and Travel Agents called the 'Tourplanner'. Each overseas office was asked to supply a photograph of anything in their area easily associated with it. They required photograph and a short article on it.

We choose the Rift Valley because it transversed Tanzania and Kenya, a very large part of our region. I was charged with securing a photograph and writing a supporting article.

I decided to call my friend Prof Leakey, the world famous anthropologist, known for his work in the 'valley'. "Well now young Denis. You must first of all understand that two quakes formed the Great Rift. One very much older than the other." said Leakey. "Hold on a second while I make notes" I requested. "Right, the first quake was when?"

"It was around 20 million years, no just a minute, it was 25. No I had better not rely on my memory, I will look up the exact dates for you. I do know that they are 22 million years apart!!"

I chipped in "Please don't worry, although I clearly understand in archaeological terms it is very important, the folk who will be reading my article, will not worry in the least bit when it took place".

THEY FOLLOWED THE TRACKS

Two Aer Lingus, Irish Airlines First Officers came to Kenya in the fifties wanting to go on a 'Hunting Safari'. When they learned of the overall costs, they decided to go it alone.

They bought their licences, hired a truck, rifles, tent, map, sleeping bags and sufficient food.

They were told, that the 'Professional Hunters' relied on trackers to locate the game.

They therefore would find and follow tracks. Not long after reaching their allocated 'hunting blocks', they found some tracks. And followed them for days seeing nothing.

Eventually, they shot a train!

Any idea why the Irish never go elephant hunting?
They get tired of carrying the heavy decoy!

LOUD MOUTH IN MUSCAT

Unfortunately, at the time there was no through connection to Nairobi from Dubai by Gulf Air. It called for a night stop at Muscat, in the evening I wished to return to my base.

With the difficulties of obtaining a visa and because the total transit time was 7 hours 30 minutes, rather than get a visa and spend what amounted to under five hours in bed, I decided to use the excellent First Class Lounge facility at Seeb International Airport Muscat.

The Lounge had lovely wide, soft leather seats and normally one could stretch out and sleep in comfort.

There must have been about six other passengers in the lounge with me trying to sleep, when a group of passengers came in to spend their 80 minutes transit. From their conversation, dominated by an American with a loud Texas accent, it was clear that they were 'oilmen'.

Some of my 'sleeping' companions, all Asians, made noises of protestation, all to no avail. I decided that the fact that I was on a staff ticket, and therefore normally debarred from complaint about revenue passengers was null and void. I owed it to my fellow passengers, to speak up.

Just as I was about to get up and firmly but politely request a cut down of the noise, the Texan said "Ya know, all that hassle we just went through would never have occurred a few years ago. We are suffering a lot with the demise of B.C.A.L. I transited this airport on God only knows how many occasions over the past years en route to Houston. Normally, the connection to B.C.A.L went like a song, Whenever our incoming flight was late and we missed B.C.A.L, they would always have someone meet us and arrange our onward flights to Houston by whoever was available, we were always given multiple choice. The idiot who met us tonight, did not even know where Houston is!"

I turned over, deciding to endure the chatter.
How could I remonstrate with such a supporter of my former airline?

MEMORY LOSS

On board a B737, an Economy Class passenger, who alone, considered himself a personal friend of the airline's chairman, full of self importance, was trying to impress his travelling companions. He was demanding sweets, newspapers and complimentary champagne in flight.

On realising that he was getting nowhere, when a female Cabin Attendant arrived with the bar trolley, he asked her "Do you know who I am? Without blinking, the lass said to one of the questioners companions "Excuse me sir, the gentleman sitting next to you has a problem. He appears to have forgotten his name, if you know him, would you mind helping him with his temporary amnesia please?"

JAMAICA RUM

My wife relates an incident of almost fatal consequences which happened in the early fifties.

When flights used to arrive in the Caribbean, free glasses of rum were on offer as both passengers and crews disembarked from their aircraft. Additionally, rum was incredibly cheap in both the shops and hotels.

As a consequence, many a crew became incredibly inebriated on the very smooth alcoholic beverage. One crew, who had a 'layover' of three days, joined another crew already in the hotel and had a virtual non stop party for two days and their first night. They became more and more boisterous and noisy. So much so, that the two female members of the crews locked and barricaded themselves in one room. The girls were literally terrified of what the men might get up to.

Their fears were well founded, a number of guests complained of the noise and abuse and the duty manager went to the 'party' demanding that they all behave and cut the noise out. The drunk mini mob not only totally ignored the duty manager, they took all the furniture out of two rooms, piled it up on the lawn and tried to set fire to it.

As well as the hotel fire service, the Hotel General Manager was informed and he went to the revellers remonstrating and insisting on more orderly behaviour.

Sadly, the participants were beyond reasoning with and to the contrary set about the General Manager. When they caught hold of him, they rolled him up in a large carpet, carried him to the pool and threw him in!
Fortunately, although the hour was very late, a number of the hotel's staff were on hand and able to dive into the pool and free their boss.

The carrier concerned very severely reprimanded and demoted every man involved.

OPTICALS

A 'well oiled' but neither speech slurred nor legless passenger boarded a flight, when 'the drinks round' reached him, he ordered a double brandy. This tipped the scales and he became very drunk.

When he finished the brandy, he asked the passenger sitting next to him, 'Hey buddy, how do I get another drink?" His companion indicating towards the overhead call button, said to him 'Press that'.
The drunk lifted his glass to just under the call button and pressed it!

THE MEXICO EARTHQUAKE

British Caledonian's 'offline' Manager Mexico was based in Mexico City at the time of the City's earthquake.

The manager relates that he was in the shower when the quake struck.

As many know, quakes have a very strange effect on one's thinking. Our man thought 'My God the children, I had better check on where and how they are'. Rushing out of the bathroom, it dawned on him that he had better put on some clothes before going out into the street. He took appropriate action.

Just as he was about to go through the front door, he glanced into the hall mirror. His clothing consisted of a 'Sou-wester, wellies and absolutely nothing else – "Silly boy" he said to himself.

PRESENTING HIS CREDENTIALS

The Ambassador of an African country, was scheduled to present his credentials to Her Majesty the Queen at Buckingham Palace,

To save any procedural embarrassment, due to the very strict etiquette and protocols, the Master of Protocol would take inexperienced diplomats through the requirements of the important ceremonial day. The ambassador was reminded of the necessity of punctuality, Her Majesty's diary being very tight and lateness cannot be accommodated. The ambassador assured his tutor, that he would be at the palace in good time.

The Master of Protocol arrived a good 20 minutes before the diplomats were due. To his surprise, he saw the African ambassador walking towards him wearing his 'top hat' upside down.

Delicately, The 'Master' hinted, that the hat was being worn the wrong way around.

Indignantly, the ambassador replied.

"Sir, I am not wearing it, I am *carrying it!*"

"THIS IS BCAL!"

My policy has always been, where possible, promote from within. It has a number of benefits, not least that of encouraging staff to believe that you really do have their interests at heart.

In Kampala Uganda, we had an excellent and very talented lady Ms Roxy Dastur, Receptionist & Telephonist. Amongst her many talents, lay her ability to produce wonderful large window displays for a fraction of the cost an 'ad' agency would charge. One must decide between making do with head office produced material which seldom fills the space available, hammering ones budget on locally commercially produced material or (if one was fortunate) utilising such talents as those of Ms Dastur which were most professional.

Roxy applied for a Reservations Agent vacancy creating a need for a new Receptionist/Telephonist. To replace Roxy, I decided to give James, our messenger/cleaner, about whom *all held* the highest opinion, a chance.

For around a week, Roxy spent every spare minute teaching James her job.

She tutored him how to operate the P.A.B.X and on the finer points of welcoming visitors. She taught him to answer every incoming telephone call, with 'a smile in his voice' and a greeting 'Good morning or Good afternoon, this is British Caledonian, may I help you?, Mr Long sir, hold on and I will put you through to his secretary'. James passed his training with flying colours.

On the first morning James was in charge of the switchboard, John Philip my friend and Managing Director of Barclays Bank Uganda, called my direct line."Denis, what the hell is going on in your organisation? he roared. John, normally the archetypal bank M.D, was full of diplomacy and tact.

Something obviously had upset him. "I have no idea, what has up set you?" I replied "My secretary has the morning off. I could not recall your direct line number and dialled the general office. I was greeted with,

'Good morning OR Good afternoon, this is British Caledonian, may I help you?"

MARBLES for TANANARIVE

After spending most of the morning at Nairobi airport, where he hoped to collect some personal goodies from Rome, our Regional Manager (R.M) returned to city office in a hell of a 'Paddy'.

I asked him "What is upsetting you?" "Bloody xyz (Manager Madagascar), he took up all four tons available cargo space.

My consignment was left behind". The R.M replied. "What on earth is he importing in such vast quantity?" I queried.

"Marbles" said the R.M

Immediately I realised that it was marble for the new office in Tananarive. I said "Marbles", why on earth does he need so many?

"For his new office" the R.M said, still most annoyed.

"What is he trying to do steal the World Championships from Tinsley Green?" (Site of the annual competition in Sussex near Gatwick Airport) I asked winding up the R.M.

"Denis, World Championships, Tinsley Green what on earth are you talking about? I donta understand you". His good English failed him when excited.

"You said that Manager Madagascar was importing four tons of marbles, that is an awful lot of marbles, why else would he import so many?"

"For his walls, he is going to stick them on his walls" said the R.M. Winding him up further, "Is he going to arrange them like a mosaic?" I said.

By this time, the R.M was at bursting point. "Denis, I am confused, he's got 4,000 kilos of the best Carrar Marbles"

"Oh, C...., you mean four tons of Marble, not marbles. Marbles are small coloured glass balls. It just like sheep. Singular SHEEP, plural SHEEP. Singular Marble, plural 4,000 kilos of Marble

The plural is the same as the singular" says I.
"English, English I'll never speak it proper! said C......
"CORRECTLY" I counselled.

ROLLS ROYCE

Late one evening at Gatwick Airport London, a breathless gentleman rushed up to the Departures 'Check In' Desks asking for a policeman. When one arrived, the gentleman panted "I have just parked my car in the Parking Lot where I saw a car collide with a brand new Rolls Royce which was correctly parked, the driver at fault drove off. The registration numbers are so and so".

The policeman called his station passing the numbers and asking for priority on the Rolls. He required the owner's name 'pronto'. In a few minutes, he had what he required.

Although the terminal was quiet, there was no response to the Public Address calls. It was decided, that the owner must be on one of the two last departing flights. They were the BR353 to Banjul, Freetown and Monrovia and the BR663 to Rio, Sao Paolo, Buenos Aires and Santiago. A quick check revealed that there was a passenger by the name of the Rolls owner on the BR663. A call was made to the appropriate 'Gate' instructing them to "hold boarding".

At the Gate, the Police made contact with the owner of the Rolls and told him of the damage to his lovely new car.

Calmly, the owner turned to them saying, "I'm off to Brazil on holiday. That's your responsibility, I will be back in 21 days" he then, without waiting for a response boarded his aircraft. The Passenger Services Duty Officer said "If it had been my new bicycle, I would have disembarked".

EPILOGUE

Sitting on the third floor verandah of our lovely (company) house in Freetown Sierra Leone, I was reminiscing over most of the foregoing anecdotes with Greg Davies a truly likeable, much younger colleague from B.C.A.L Head Office Cargo. Greg summed up my airline life with "Boy do I envy you and Bill Rothera". "Why?" somewhat surprised, I asked. Greg replied "You and Bill, have lived through what must undoubtedly be the most exciting, funny and enjoyable period of commercial aviation. While still a great industry, in which to be employed, there certainly is not today, anything like the camaraderie and atmosphere in what clearly has been a great labour of love for you two".

I do not know too much about today, at either Head Office or a truly big airport such as London, where each is required to stick to a given job. I do know, having spent three-quarters of my working life overseas, that team work is the essential ingredient of an overseas assignment, particularly in the developing world. As such, it draws all sections and departments very close together.

I have so far, written in excess of 650 anecdotes and have a host of photographs, cartoons and sketches. Twelve friends, six from within and six from without the industry, have read and 'graded' each anecdote. I had hoped to select the consensus opinion on which were the best stories, because of the great diversity of humour and opinion it became an impossibility. However, if you enjoy reading that selected for **'LONG ODDS'** half as much as I have enjoyed writing and publishing it, anticipate **'LONGER ODDS', 'EVEN LONGER ODDS'** and **'LONGEST ODDS'** in the not too far distant future.

My most sincere thanks go to all, at B.C.A.L Head Office and overseas, and interline colleagues, far to numerous to mention, who have enriched my life in the *most* fascinating of industries.

GLOSSARY of TERMS

I have tried to avoid the use of airline abbreviations and jargon to ensure easier reading and understanding. However, where used refer below.

A

A.C.U	Air Conditioning Unit.
A.M	Area Manager.
A.O.G	Aircraft On Ground (Unservicable-sick).
A.P.M	Airport Manager.
A & P	Advertising & Publicity.
ASAP (asap)	As Soon As Possible.
A.T.P.L	Air Transport Pilot Licence. Cpts & S.F.Os
A & Prom	Advertising & Promotions.
A.T.A	Actual Time of Arrival.
A.T.C	Air Traffic Control or Controller.
A.T.D	Actual Time of Departure.
A.T.V	Airways Terminal Victoria.
A.T	Air Terminal.

<u>AIRCRAFT TYPES</u> *by manufacturer.*

<u>BRITISH AIRCRAFT CORPORATION -BRITISH AEROSPACE</u>

BAC 1-11	Short Medium Haul 2 engine jet.
VC10 & S.VC10	Long Haul 4 engine jet.

<u>BRITTEN NORMAN (PILATUS)</u>

BNT TRISLANDER	Short Haul 3 engine propeller.

<u>BOEING</u>

B707	Long Haul 4 engine jet.
B727	Short-Medium Haul 3 engine jet.
B737	Short-Medium Haul 2 engine jet.
B747	Long Haul 4 engine jet.
B757	Medium-Short Haul 2 engine jet.
B767	Long Haul 2 engine jet.

N.B
757 has a single aisle, whereas **767** larger, has a double aisle.

<u>DOUGLAS (DC) & Mc DONALD DOUGLAS (MD)</u>

DC3	Short-Medium Haul 2 engine propeller.

DC4/ARGONAUT	Long Haul 4 engine propeller.
CANADAIR DC4	with pressurisation unit loosing 6 seats.
DC6	Long Haul 4 engine propeller.
DC7	Long Haul 4 engine Tbo/propeller.
DC8	Long Haul 4 engine jet.
DC9	Medium- Short Haul 2 engine jet.
MD80 & 83	Medium- Short Haul 2 engine jet.
Stretched DC9	
DC10-10	Medium Haul 3 engine jet.
DC10-30	Long Haul 3 engine jet.
MD11	Long Haul 3 engine jet.

LOCKHEED

CONSTELLATION	Long Haul 4 Engine propeller.
ELECTRA.	Medium Haul 4 Engine propeller.
STRETCHED	This means that a version of an aircraft is made longer.
	e.g. The **VC10** had about 13' added to the fuselage and higher capacity fuel tank wings to become a **Super VC10.**

AIRLINE CODING

AA	American Airlines	**AW**	America West.
AI	Air India.	**AF**	Air France.
AR	Aerolineas Argentinas.	**AC**	Air Canada.
AN	Ansett (Australia).	**AZ**	Alitalia Italy.
AY	Finnair.		
BA	B.O.A.C/Bri Airways.	**BE**	British European A-ways.
BM	British Midland.	**BR**	British Caledonian.
BN	Brannif (U.S.A).		
CP	Canadian Pacific Airlines.	**CX**	Cathay Pacific.
CO	Continental Airlines.		
DA	Dan Air.(London).	**DL**	Delta. (U.S.A)
EK	Emirates (Dubai).	**ET**	Ethiopian Airlines.
EI	Aer Lingus (Eire).	**EC**	East African Airlines.
GF	Gulf Air.		
IC	Indian Airlines Corp.		
JL	Japan Airlines.		
KQ	Kenya Airways.	**KL**	K.L.M (Holland).
LH	Lufthansa (Germany).		
MS	Msarair (Now Egyptair).		

NW	North West Airlines (U.S.A).		
OA	Olympic Airways.	**OS**	Austrian Airlines.
PA	Pan American.	**PK**	Pakistan International Airlines.
PL	Phillipines Airlines.		
QF	QANTAS Australia.	**QM**	Air Malawi.
QZ	Zambia Airways.		
RG	Varig Brazil.	**RO**	TAROM Romania.
SA	South African Airways.	**SN**	S.A.B.E.N.A Belgium.
SK	Scandinavian Airlines System.	**SR**	Swissair.
SU	Aeroflot Russia.		
*TE	Air New Zealand.	**TP**	Air Portugal.
TH	Thai Airways.	**TW**	Trans World Airways.
UA	United Airlines.	**UM**	Air Zimbabwe.
UT	U.T.A France.		
VA	Viasa Venezuela.		
WT	Nigerian Airways.		
UK & E	U.K & Europe.	**UK & Er**	U.K & Eire.

changed to **NZ since merger of N.Z. National & Air New Zealand.*

B

B.H.C	British High Commissioner.
	D/B.H.C (Deputy)

C

C.A.A	Civil Aviation Authority. (British).
C.A.T	Clear Air Turbulence.
C.o.G	Centre of Gravity.
COMMANDER	Aircraft captain.
Cpt	Captain.
Chief	Chief Steward.
CLOSE OFF	Time flight stops accepting further payload.
C.S.D	Cabin Service Director.
C.S.M	Cabin Staff Member.
C.T.O	City Ticket Office.

D

D.C.A	Director / Directorate of Civil Aviation.

E

E.R   Eastern Routes.
E.T.A   Estimated Time of Arrival.
E.T.D   Estimated Time of Departure

F

F.A.A   Federal Aviation Agency (U.S.A).
F/At   Flight Attendant.
F.B.A   Free Baggage Allowance.
F/E   Flight Engineer.
F/O & S/F/O   First Officer. & Senior F/O.holds A.T.P.L
F/C   First Class.
F.M.C   Initials of manufacturer of a **High Loader.** Motorised unit for loading/offloading containers of baggage & cargo
FLIGHTIE   Senior Flight Hostess (Purser).
F.M   Frequency Modulated.

G

G.M   General Manager.
GOCON   Ramp Control Manager (gives 'GO'signal).
G.S.M   General Sales Manager.

H

HARMAATAN   Is a phenomena known principally to West Africa. Sahara dust storms rage across the desert lifting dust to great heights, it is carried thousands of miles. When it collides with fresh winds off the ocean, the dust falls forming a type of fog. A considerable hazard to aircraft approaching an airport.
H.F   High Frequency radio transceiver.
HOSTIE   Stewardess or Air Hostess.

I

'ID'   Identification card with photo and details of holder.
INTERLINE   From one airline to another. Passengers-Cargo.

170

J

J/C Business Class.

K

K.A.S Kensington Air Station.

L

LAYOVER. Crew rest point when away from base.
Load Master Cargo Officer responsible for all loading.
Load Message Message containing details of commercial payload. Sent by airport to all points ahead.

M

M.A.Rs Mid Atlantic Routes.
MOCON Movement Control Manager.

N

N.A.S North Atlantic Routes.
N.O Navigation Officer.

P

P.A Public Address.
P/A Personal Assistant.
PORT side Left side of aircraft or ship.
Pur Purser.

R

REBATES

R1-N1-S1 Confirmed space.
R2-N2-S2 Space Available.
'ID% Industry at indicated % (100, 90, 80, 50 + status).
'AD% Agents at indicated % (100,75,50 + status).

R.M Regional Manager.

S

S.A.Rs South Atlantic Routes.
S.C.S.M Senior Cabin Staff Member.

'SICK'	Aircraft unserviceable (un-well – sick).
Slip/ 'On Slip	Crew layover point away from base.
SITA	Airlines owned international (telex type).
	communications system (worlds largest).
SITA PRIORITIES	QX-QU-QK+QD which is the basic charge.
S.T.D	Scheduled Time of Departure.
STARBOARD side	Right side of aircraft or ship.

T

TIME

am is normal print   **24 hour clock is in bold.**

(1)	**0100**	(2)	**0200**	(3)	**300**	(4)	**0400**
(5)	**0500**	(6)	**0600**	(7)	**0700**	(8)	**0800**
(9)	**0900**	(10)	**1000**	(11)	**1100**	(12)	**1200**

pm is in normal print   **24 hour clock is in bold.**

(1)	**1300**	(2)	**1400**	(3)	**1500**	(4)	**1600**
(5)	**1700**	(6)	**1800**	(7)	**1900**	(8)	**2000**
(9)	**2100**	(10)	**2200**	(11)	**2300**	(12)	**2400**

Midnight is known to professionals as **2359** or **0001** to differentiate date.
2400 is not used. Minutes are added to hour.
e.g.. **1305** is 1.05pm, **1347** is 1.47 pm. **0237** is 2.37am, **0840** is 8.40am.

T'/C	Tourist Class.

U

U.H.F	Ultra High Frequency radio transceiver.

V

V.H.F	Very High Frequency radio transceiver.

W

WAITLIST	List of passengers or cargo on waiting list.

Y

Y/C	Economy Class.